THE
SPORTSMAN

THE
SPORTSMAN

STEPHEN HARRIS

Photographs by Toby Glanville

Φ

The History

The Recipes

The End

Foreword

It was food that first lured me to Whitstable, at the time a rather unloved little seaside town crouched along its pebbly shore. (This was before we Brits reignited our love for our indigenous beaches, and beach huts and bunting became unlikely contenders for the chicest of accessories.) The Royal Native Oyster Stores had opened in a handsome, ramshackle building right on the shore, fulfilling every city dweller's fantasy of a simpler life, lit by stunning sunsets, albeit one embellished by the briny slurp of native oysters, the excitement of being allowed to order chips with lobsters and buckets of chilled Muscadet sur lie.

I gave up on the Oyster Stores rather quickly. For one thing, it became very much 'discovered'; for another, I'd made a discovery of my own, past the caravan parks and little shops selling buckets and spades in far bleaker Seasalter. 'Grotty rundown pub by the sea,' is The Sportsman's self-mocking Twitter bio, but back at the turn of the millennium, it really was a little... well, scruffy is putting it kindly, and not in an artfully distressed way. The old pub hunkered down in its unphotogenic car park surrounded by marshland, and with the Thames Estuary hidden behind a sea wall. Stephen Harris was always in the kitchen. A bearded man would glower at you as you arrived, no doubt infuriated by ramblers and twitchers demanding soup and a nice crusty roll. (This was Stephen's brother Phillip; he has cheered up enormously over the intervening years.)

The menu, scrawled on a blackboard by the bar, gastropub-style, wasn't a long one. I think the first thing I ever ordered here was called 'crispy duck', and I anticipated some kind of riff on the Chinese restaurant classic. What I didn't expect was something so perfectly gorgeous, with its burnished, Pringle-crisp skin and melting, confit meat, its accompaniments of cool, cultured soured cream and the sting of homemade chilli sauce. As I ate, my eyes grew rounder. Now this, this was a find. I immediately became a devoted and committed fan.

Each time I returned, The Sportsman got better, even though the bar was pretty high in the first place. Stephen (he's one of the very few chefs I know IRL, as our internet chums would say, so I feel I can call him by his first name) is the classic autodidact, pushing his creativity and enthusiasms further and further, reaching forever for some kind of perfection. He's a magpie, and a super-creative one: he travels to the world's greatest restaurants, absorbing their influences and – I'm aware I run the risk of coming across like an 'X Factor' judge here – making them very much his own. His 'Rockpool': the clearest, sparkling broth, rippling with the umami of dashi, in which bob the sweetest fruits of the sea, both animal and vegetal. Or a play on René Redzepi's notorious 'Flowerpot', but entirely Kentish. Or Michel Bras' 'Gargouillou de jeunes légumes' reinvented as 'Salmagundi', a horticultural extravaganza of seasonal vegetables and freshly picked herbs. He's not one of those chefs you suspect might need to get out more. But in recent years he has drawn his horns back in, thrilling to the joys of simplicity and locality. Stephen's kitchen now delivers food that tastes quite bracingly of itself, with a revelatory purity and brightness. It's the sort of cooking that looks simple, but is, in fact, fiendishly difficult to achieve.

This is unequivocally good news. Nobody can doubt Stephen's ability to pull off the flashy stuff, but his dishes now tell a story of his immediate surroundings: the salt marsh lamb from the neighbouring fields; the crab from the waters that lap the shingle mere metres from the pub's front door, with vast, ripe quantities of it laced through a supremely creamy risotto; his own home-cured ham, salty and pungent and porcine in an almost primeval way, the product of an initiative undertaken long before today's bearded, tattooed young guns got themselves their own curing rooms. The salt is extracted from Seasalter seawater; the name gives it away – the village was historically a centre for salt production. Stephen's intelligence informs the tiniest details.

Even the house-churned cultured butter is just completely beautiful: I would happily travel across the country for this and the bread – oh my lord, the bread – alone. But then I'd be missing out on the oysters (it was here that I had my first experience of the bivalves topped with a small frazzle of the kitchen's own-made chorizo); or Stephen's play on fried lamb breast Ste Menehould, crisp and fatty and luscious, for dunking into a spiky, resonant mint sauce. And the famous slip sole in its bath of seaweed butter, a menu stalwart, its firm, meaty flesh peeling away to leave a cartoon fishbone: ungarnished, startling in its starkness, brave and brilliant. Part of Stephen Harris's genius is his ability to let food tell its own story. He's a romantic that way.

The Harrises have never been ones to blow their own trumpets. Stephen once said to me, 'I plan to die without ever having written a cookbook.' (I'll pause here for a bit of a guffaw.) They've been hesitant to point out their pioneering work on foraging, on seasonality, on locavorism, all the badges of the clued-up contemporary kitchen. Or to take credit for the very welcome current trend for an unbuttoned, un-tableclothed approach to (dreaded phrase) 'fine dining' with friendly, knowledgeable staff who don't fill you with posh-restaurant anxiety. So I'm more than happy to toot it for them. Loudly.

Of course, it's not my secret any more. The critics have come in their droves, as have the gastrotourists. It has become a place of culinary pilgrimage, a little less scruffy, true, but still deliciously informal and accessible, one of the few places on the planet I'm happy to sit back and wallow in an hours-long, multi-course tasting menu lunch while the sun moves over the pub's roof, until one of the famous Whitstable sunsets does its technicolour thing. When, in 2008, The Sportsman was awarded a Michelin star, Stephen told me: 'People said to me, "Well, we thought it was good", like they needed validation of their own opinions.' I didn't need Messieurs Michelin to point that out to me: I've gone on record as saying this is my favourite place to eat in the British Isles. I can't imagine that changing any time soon.

Marina O'Loughlin

Opening Night

November 1999

Nothing could have prepared me for the feelings I experienced on the opening night of The Sportsman.

We had taken the keys to the building on Monday 1 November 1999, and spent the next week ripping out the layers of crap that had accrued over the years. The Sportsman had been a hotel for shooting parties in the early twentieth century, and then in the 1950s it became a drinking place for caravanning tourists until everybody started to holiday abroad. There was no village around it. It stood alone on a salt marsh four miles from Whitstable.

I realised we were in a position to grow gradually because we didn't owe any money to the banks. To begin the work, we had borrowed £20,000 from our brother Damian, whose record label, Skint, was doing very well.

There were old beer-stained carpets, cheap banquettes and even sheets of chipboard covering broken windows. The net curtains that had hidden customers from the outside world were taken down, and even on the first morning a new building had started to emerge. It was like a sleeping giant awakening. The building underneath was starting to breathe, and it looked like our gamble would pay off, as an unexpectedly colonial interior began to reveal itself.

This optimism on the first day was quickly checked by the realisation of what needed to be done. The floor had to be replaced, for starters, and the whole building had to be cleaned and painted from top to bottom. My brother Philip had put together a group of friends who had the skills needed to carry out the renovation, and I still remember that week fondly. A sense of teamwork and camaraderie meant that the time flew by, and the looming terror of being left alone to actually run the business could be put to the back of my mind.

I spent the week in the kitchen throwing out domestic units and deep fat fryers. The only equipment worth keeping was the pass, and we actually still have that today. Everything else had to go, and it was energising to strip the kitchen back to just four clean white walls and a newly painted floor.

I went over to France with Philip and bought the equipment we would need from a kitchen supplier. Everything was so much cheaper over there that we managed to equip the kitchen for £5,000: this included a range cooker, service fridge, sink units, pots, pans and utensils.

I had been to Stoke in the Midlands of England to buy plates from the seconds shops at the major potteries, too. This was in keeping with my idea of a budget top restaurant – we would use the same plates as the posh, expensive places, but would buy the ever-so-slightly imperfect seconds from Spode and Wedgewood. I just loved the idea of a seconds restaurant. That a bowl or plate might have a small dent or bubble in it, but it was fundamentally the same as the very expensive version. This was the blueprint.

Six days later, we had the inside of the pub finished in time to open and welcome a few friends on the Saturday night. It was a very rewarding drink amid the smell of new wood and paint – we had achieved an incredible amount in the week since we took over. That night I found myself behind the bar when the phone rang: it was someone wanting to book a table, and I realised that we had forgotten to buy a diary to take bookings. We were so close to the wire with the budget that I decided we would just make do, and grabbed my own diary. That was our stop-gap for a few days while we sorted one out.

It wasn't until the Tuesday night that reality set in – we were finally open for food. I remember standing outside the pub looking at the distant twinkling lights of Whitstable and wondering why anyone would leave the comfort of their living rooms and come out to the middle of nowhere on a freezing-cold night to eat in a pub. What with the excitement of the opening and all of the preparations I hadn't thought about it from that angle. Luckily a couple of tables – friends of friends – had decided to brave the weather, and I cooked in The Sportsman for the first time.

Watercress soup with oysters, pot-roast pork with sage roasting juices, and hot chocolate pudding were my three stand-out dishes from that night. It felt quite lonely working in a kitchen on my own, and even now the sound of Moby's album *Play* can transport me back to that period of stomach-churning nerves before each service. When I had finished the washing up, late that Tuesday evening, I contemplated the situation. The only way that people would venture out on a winter's night was because the food was so good that they had to. The food must be that good. These people would then tell their friends about the amazing meal they had eaten, and word would spread from there. No advertising, no marketing but the purest form of growth – word of mouth.

Learning to Cook

September 1992

My first meal in a Michelin-starred restaurant set the tone for how I taught myself to cook. It was a meal at a place called Chez Nico, at 90 Park Lane, in September 1992. It had two stars and although I was a good amateur cook, I didn't know that such perfection was possible.

Everything was clean and bright, the food was powerful but balanced, and my reaction was simply: I must find out how they do this. Even at that first great meal I can remember thinking it was a shame that most people would never experience such good food because it was so expensive. The whole world of fine dining was, almost deliberately, priced out of the range of ordinary people: I looked at the essentials. It was basically a piece of fish or meat, a sauce and some vegetables on a plate. Everything else was just dressing – the *amuse bouche*, the sommelier, the pre-dessert and petit fours – none of these things were essential to the main event. When I was at school, one of my history teachers had written that I was too quick to see the central issue and needed to demonstrate how I had reached my conclusion. Well, here I was doing it again, but this time it was a good instinct.

Then the strangest thing happened. I had a dinner party on the Saturday night that followed this meal, and I decided to try and copy the food I had eaten. I cooked a raviolo of salmon, a main course that I can't remember, and lemon tart for pudding. My friends Neil and Sasha were quite astonished, and I have to admit that I was too. I had cooked something to a level that I wasn't capable of the day before.

With the memory of the meal at Chez Nico's still fresh in my mind, I knew how far I had to take the flavours. For example, I made a velouté of chives, now understanding that the reduction of the stock and vermouth was essential to the underlying power of the sauce, and the vital role of lemon, which stopped the sauce from being unctuous, lifting and broadening the flavour. The chives, when chopped and added at the last minute, remained vivid green and retained the vegetal quality of their taste. I realised that I could teach myself to cook – with the great chefs of London as my unwitting teachers.

Over the next few months and years, I bought the cookbooks of Nico Ladenis, Pierre Koffman, Marco Pierre White, and then went for many meals at their restaurants. Afterwards, I would go home and copy the things I had been eating. I was quite methodical as I worked my way through any book that might help, such as Julia Child's *Mastering the Art of French Cooking*. I used her book to learn about the different types of pastry and sauces, and I can remember taking all day to make a veal stock that I then reduced down to a *demi-glace*. This elevated the results of my cooking to new levels, to the point where friends would tell me I should open a restaurant. But I wasn't getting carried away, because I knew how these things work. Of course, your friends will always tell you how good you are – when I was in a band, my friends were very supportive and said we were great, but I didn't believe it. I needed to find a way of checking whether I was deluded or not.

I can remember a programme from the late nineties on Channel 4 whereby an amateur took over a restaurant for the night. In this early reality show, the amateur was so arrogant before the night and so utterly defeated by the end of it that I knew I had a lot to learn. The thousand-yard stare as he contemplated the fact that he was not as good as he thought he was, made worse by having to confront this hard truth in front of millions of people, was a chastening watch. I realised that if I ever wanted to have a restaurant I would have to start at the bottom as a commis chef and work my way up.

When I first took on Dan Flavell, our head chef, after The Sportsman had been open for six months, I realised that the way I had learnt to cook was also a great way to teach. I took him to the top restaurants in London, which at the time were Aubergine, under (Gordon Ramsay), Pétrus and Richard Corrigan's Lindsay House among others, to teach him the flavours I aspired to. When we got back into the kitchen we had the memory of great restaurant kitchens guiding us – and we've used this method of learning ever since.

Becoming a Chef

April 1995

I was driving down from London for a lunch in Surrey with my friend Linsey. We were going to a restaurant that belonged to her family friend, and it was called Bryce's at the Old School House in Ockley. I had already decided that I couldn't carry on in my current job as a financial advisor and was trying decide what to do, so my future career formed the main topic of conversation on our journey.

I had two ideas: either try to build a career as a journalist, or become a chef. I had very good media contacts, as many of my clients as a financial advisor worked in this area, and I had done a few shifts on *The Guardian* and *The Independent*. I was leaning towards journalism.

Linsey came from a food-loving family and had grown up on the King's Road in Chelsea, London. With the kind of confidence that growing up in a place like that gives you, she thought nothing about going to multi-Michelin-starred restaurants. It was her talking about the food of Nico Ladenis that had encouraged me to go to Chez Nico for that life-changing meal three years earlier. Linsey was going out with Michael, a good friend of mine from university days, and we would often have dinner parties where Lindsey and I would try to out cook each other while Michael would organise the wine. We also went on holiday with a large group of friends and cooked great meals where we all took turns to cook.

Linsey, a great cook herself, seemed to think that I had a real talent and was trying to encourage me to become a chef. I was a bit less gung-ho and doubted whether I could make it, especially as I was starting so late.

When the owner of the restaurant, a giant Scot called Billy Bryce, came over to chat with us during the meal, Linsey blurted out 'This is Stephen. He wants to be a chef but isn't sure, can he come and try out in your kitchen?'

I wonder if I would ever have become a chef if it wasn't for Linsey being so forward and Billy being so generous. 'Of course' he said. 'Come and work for me for a week and I guarantee that by Wednesday you will know the answer.'

He was right, the moment came on Wednesday afternoon when I was working in his kitchen on my own. I was doing some prep on the pastry section and I had a sudden realisation that this didn't feel like work. I was being paid to do something that I usually did for free. It hit me almost like a religious conversion.

Although it was going to be the more difficult option, I knew then that I had to become a chef. The hours would be long, the pay terrible, and — to the rest of the youngsters in the kitchen — I was that strange bloke in his thirties who wanted to do this tough, backbreaking job.

When my time at Billy's came to an end, I went back to London and wondered how on earth I was going to break into the world of food. The day I got back I looked in the jobs section of the *Evening Standard* and saw an advert for a restaurant called the Fire Station that I had been to and loved just months before. The advert was asking for people without any professional experience but who were very good cooks and fancied a job as a chef. This was getting spooky...

I went to the interview and met Eugene, the acting head chef, and Neil, the sous chef. The very talented head chef was leaving the restaurant, and these two had the job finding new hires. At the time, they had a guy who was an accountant and used to come in on Monday nights just for fun. He was a good home cook and just wanted to see what it was like in a professional kitchen. Eugene and Neil realised that his intelligence and knowledge more than made up for his lack of experience as a chef, and this had led to them putting the advert in the paper.

They looked at me with the same sideways glance that I would get used to over the next couple of years; I think people thought I was joking or maybe had a hidden camera as it seemed so unlikely that I would be willing to work for £8,000 a year as a commis chef.

Although the restaurant was in chaos, short staffed and suffering from losing its best man, it was perfect for me to learn. I would go home at night and study my Harold McGee *On Food and Cooking* book to make sure I was ready for the jobs I would do the next day.

I realised that I was a strange person for them to have to deal with, but the kindness and warmth I got from Billy, Eugene and Neil meant that I was well on my way to becoming a chef.

MON 3	TUES 4	WEDS 5	THURS 6	FRI 7	SAT 8	SUN 9
SHEL EM	•SHEL GRACE EMILY IMOGEN HANNAH	•SHEL IMOGEN SOPHIE GRACE PHOEBE	•SHEL GRACE SOPHIE PHOEBE HANNAH –LINES	HANNAH SOPHIE PAUL EMILY IMOGEN	•EMMA EMILY PHOEBE PAUL HANNAH	GRACE PHOEBE SOPHIE CHARL CATH
	SHEL AD •GRACE CASSY PHOEBE IMOGEN EMILY	•SHEL AD SOPHIE PAUL EMILY •HANNAH	•HANNAH PAUL SOPHIE PHOEBE CATH	•GRACE SOPHIE IMOGEN PHOEBE	•EMMA GRACE EMILY SOPHIE	SARAH

MON 10	TUES 11	WEDS 12	THURS 13	FRI 14 EASTER	SAT 15	SUN 16
SHEL EM	SHEL GRACE PHOEBE IMOGEN SOPHIE	•GRACE HANNAH EMILY SOPHIE PHOEBE –LINES	•SHEL HANNAH GRACE SOPHIE PHOEBE	•SHEL GRACE IMOGEN EMILY SOPHIE GEORGE	NO HANNAH EMMA EMILY PHOEBE IMOGEN PAUL SHEL	•GRACE CHARL EMILY CATH GEORGE
	SHEL AD •HANNAH CASSY IMOGEN CATHERINE PHOEBE	HANNAH EMILY PHOEBE SOPHIE	•HANNAH PAUL SOPHIE CASSY PHOEBE	•GRACE IMOGEN CATH SOPHIE PAUL	•EMMA EMILY GRACE SOPHIE	SARAH GEORGE

MON 17 EASTER MONDAY	TUES 18	WEDS 19	THURS 20	FRI 21	SAT 22 NO EMMA	SUN 23
SHEL G	•SHEL GRACE IMOGEN PHOEBE EMILY	•GRACE HANNAH SOPHIE EMILY PHOEBE	•SHEL HANNAH GRACE SOPHIE PHOEBE	•SHEL EMILY PHOEBE HANNAH SOPHIE	•SHEL EMILY PHOEBE IMOGEN PAUL	•GRACE SOPHIE PHOEBE HANNAH CATH
	SHEL AD •GRACE CASSY SOPHIE IMOGEN PAUL	•HANNAH SOPHIE PHOEBE EMILY	HANNAH PAUL IMOGEN SOPHIE CASSY	•GRACE PHOEBE IMOGEN PAUL	•GRACE SOPHIE EMILY IMOGEN	SARAH

Finding The Sportsman

December 1998

I'm not sure I believe in light-bulb moments. They are too convenient for telling stories and unlikely to be so neatly tied up as to be the true history. However, I have to admit that the day I knew the long wait to find a suitable premises for my project was over could be described as such.

My friend Paul Mattocks used to come over to my house on Boxing Day every year at that time. I looked forward to it, as I find Christmas can get quite claustrophobic, and we would always try to go for a drive into the countryside. This year Paul had turned up in a blue MG Midget and we decided to take down the roof just to blow away a few cobwebs. As we headed out into the Kent countryside we talked – well, shouted at each other really, above the din of the wind – about what we had been up to.

Paul had been one of my best friends since I was thirteen years old. At school, he was a top student getting straight As in his Physics, Maths and Chemistry exams. He had a great career in science in front of him, probably via Oxford or Cambridge. There was just one problem – he was living his parents' dream, but not his. He decided to give up science and enrolled on a foundation art course, eventually ending up at Wimbledon and Saint Martin's art schools studying sculpture. A lot of people thought he was mad to completely change direction and turn his back on something he was so obviously good at, but he had to be true to himself.

Paul was quite typical of my friends: they were awkward, unwilling to do the obvious and still influenced by the punk attitude of our youth. We were sixteen years old in 1976, and it felt like we had just been waiting for something like punk to come along. The sixties were long gone, and the energy and attitude, which had created so many great bands, was missing from music in the seventies. Most live music had largely gone from the small clubs to massive stadiums, and the stars felt so distant as to make them irrelevant to us. We didn't want triple albums of abstract noodling, we wanted three-minute, fast, catchy singles, so when punk came along we were ready. Paul and I listened to the MC5, The Stooges, the Pretty Things and the Downliners Sect, and went to see pub rock bands like Eddie and the Hot Rods and Dr. Feelgood. I remember my brother Chris coming home from work with an article from the *NME* headlined 'Don't look over your shoulder, but the Sex Pistols are coming'. It felt like the revolution had begun.

The feeling I had about music in 1976 was similar to how I felt about restaurants in 1998. Why was it so expensive to open a restaurant – surely all you really needed was a building and a stove? Just like the music industry in the late seventies, the restaurant industry had begun to feel bloated and disconnected. If you stripped away all of the unnecessary stuff it could just be about what was on the plate – the food version of a perfect three-minute pop song.

People would often say they were disappointed that I hadn't really achieved my potential, but Paul, because of his experience, was very encouraging. My head was full of the plans I had for starting a restaurant.

By this time, I had left London after working in a few restaurants, and moved back to Whitstable. My walk to work was just 10 minutes past the harbour, along the sea front and into the beautiful old oyster warehouse that sat on Whitstable beach. I worked with a good group of people and was enjoying myself. It felt like such a long way from my old life in London and underground journeys to work. I wasn't sure that going back to that was what I really wanted.

We headed to a village pub called The Chequers in Doddington and we sat and talked more – mainly about my plans. I explained that I was having trouble finding a location to open my restaurant, and had been to look at a number of properties including the old Labour club, under the railway arches in Whitstable, a curry house in Harbour Street, and then another place in the town, where an old colleague had just pipped me to the post.

As we left Doddington we made our way back home on the road from Faversham to Whitstable. We were about to pass The Sportsman, which was something of a local landmark, when Paul decided to pull in for another quick drink.

We parked in the large, empty car park and walked into the bar. It was very dark, the carpet was a bit sticky and for some reason there was chipboard over some of the windows to block out any light. This was still a time when people who drank during the day in a pub should be protected from detection by frosted glass, often with the brewery name etched onto it.

The bar was also empty, which was understandable given the surly reaction to our presence. We sat in the back bar, and as Paul continued to talk, I realised I wasn't listening. I was looking around the room, imagining what it would look like if you stripped it right back. I looked around at the size of the building and thought about its location. Although it was in the middle of nowhere, it was very close to Whitstable, which had become a bit of a magnet for seafood lovers and media types due to the restaurant on the beach where I was working. If anything put me off, it was the size of the place. I had wanted my own small restaurant where I could cook exactly what I wanted – food with real ambition. This space would require a little more than that. But I had no doubt in my mind that I had found the perfect site; the next ten months would be spent trying to secure the lease until opening night, where the story began on 1 November 1999.

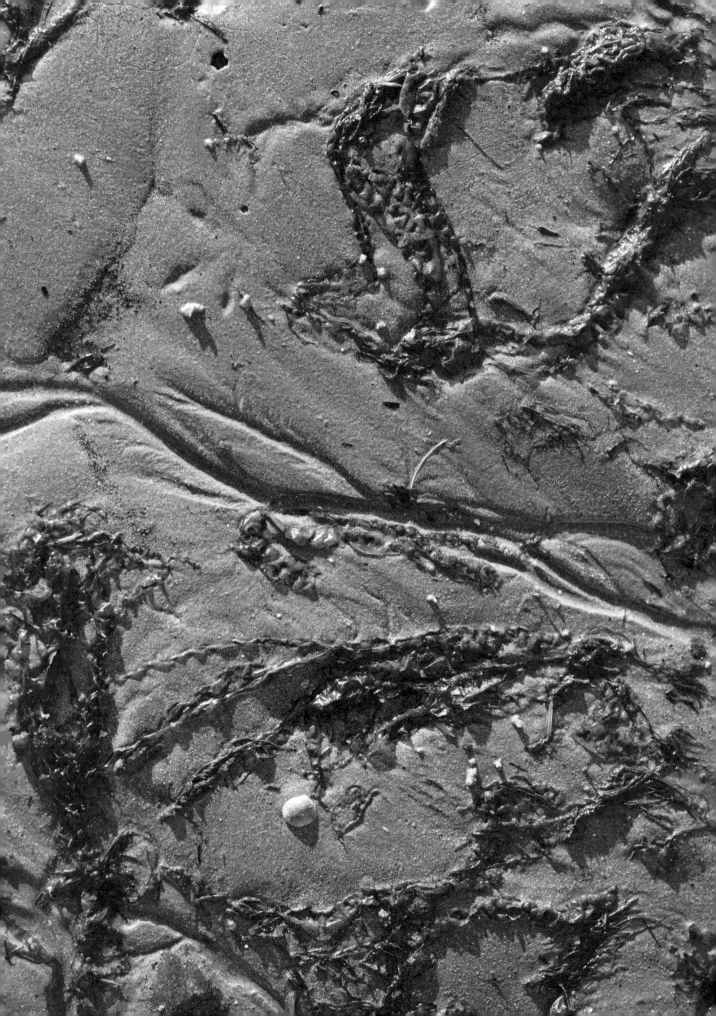

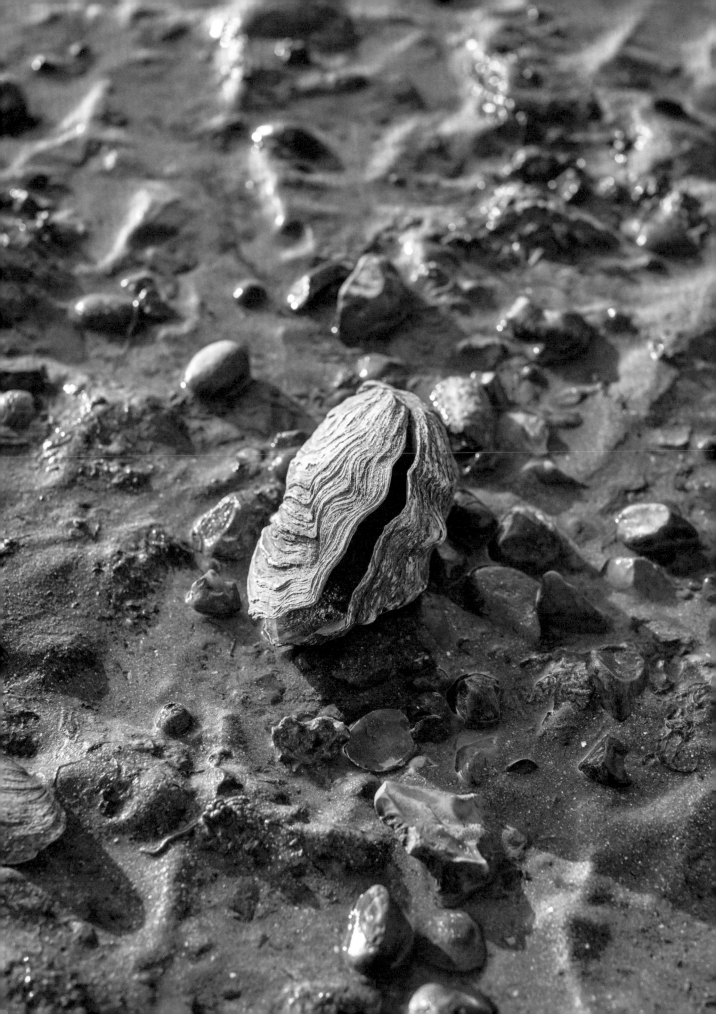

A Style of My Own

In the early days of The Sportsman, I was continuing with the same system that I had used to teach myself how to cook. I would go to the best restaurants in London and then copy and adapt dishes or ideas that I had eaten.

The players on the London scene had changed over the years, but my system had remained the same. It worked well because it meant that I was bringing the best of London to a small town. This gave the feeling to our customers that they were eating something new that no other local restaurant was serving. A lot of these were still stuck in provincial restaurant mode whereby the rules were set. Food must be very hot (too hot to taste); everywhere had to serve steak and chips; and all main courses came with microwaved vegetables, preferably from Kenya.

When we broke these rules people, would get very upset. I can remember a man walking out on a Friday night because we didn't do steak. I actually confronted him in the car park and let him know how pathetic he was. I find men who moan about food ridiculous because they are always the type who can't cook. They act like children having a tantrum because they cant get their own way. The fact was we didn't serve steak and chips because I knew, even with my limited experience, that everybody would order it, and so I would be frying chips for the rest of my life. I just didn't want to do that. Besides, I couldn't find any steak worth serving.

So our style was set. I would take ideas from the great chefs in London and adapt them to the ingredients I had available. We had some good farms around us and I would source as much from them as possible, creating a kind of cuisine de *terroir*. After a few years of this I realised that I had to develop a style of my own. I had started to travel abroad to eat at great restaurants, and I soon realised that the best chefs had a specific style or originality about their food.

Take for example Olivier Roellinger, who's based in Cancale on the Normandy-Brittany border. Before taking the decision in 2008 to turn in his Michelin stars, he had a three-star restaurant that served the ingredients of his area but with the added twist of using the local port of Saint Malo as his inspiration. Drawing on its position on one of the main spice routes, he created dishes including his famous lobster with cocoa and sherry vinegar. The spice mixes he made were vibrant and original, leading to a style of food that was familiar enough to keep it rooted but modern enough to feel exciting.

The other thing I noticed during my visit to Roellinger's restaurant was that he was using a lot of similar ingredients to the ones I had available at Seasalter. Oysters, turbot, seaweed, butter – we shared the same sea and a similar climate but he had found this interesting angle using the history of the spice trade.

Still in France, I went to Michel Bras's restaurant who pioneered the use of the unusual plants in the landscape of the Aubrac, serving them in his stunning glass-fronted restaurant overlooking the place the ingredients had come from. I was struck by how similar the landscape was to the one around us in Kent and this was enough to confirm that I should use my unique surroundings as the inspiration for the next phase of The Sportsman.

Kentish Terroir

The term *terroir* causes all sorts of problems. Some British people seem almost offended that the English language doesn't have a word that fits the bill. And I sometimes think that French people try to mystify the subject in an attempt to make it more difficult for us culinarily challenged English to understand.

So why is the word *terroir* so important to explain what we do at The Sportsman? *Terroir* can have several meanings. In the traditional context of wine, it is a way of explaining why one region's wine will differ from another even if it is made from the same grape. For example, a Chardonnay grown in Chablis will taste very different from one grown in Languedoc. To explain this we have to understand the soil, the rock that lies beneath the soil, the climate and local factors, such as the shape of the landscape. This can affect the microclimate to such an extent that a field in Burgundy can produce different wine from its neighbour, even though they are so close to each other.

If you don't believe this is possible, then you have to explain to me why a bottle of Romanée-Conti that was grown in a field in the village of Vosne in Burgundy will cost about £10,000, when a bottle grown in a field next door costs £100. Obviously, rarity and prestige have a part to play – but the gap is too big to justify without looking at the *terroir*.

In the world of food, *terroir* helps to explain why one region has a different style of food to another. Take the distinctive cuisines of Normandy and Provence. Normandy has lush pasture and, as a result, a lot of dishes are cooked in butter or cream. The moderate climate is good for growing apples, pears and grazing lamb (especially on the coast) while the fish will come from the Channel or Atlantic. In Provence, the climate is Mediterranean, which means that olive oil is the main fat. Lemons, tomatoes and peppers abound, and the fish comes from the warmer waters of the Mediterranean. Goats (and actually sheep) thrive too, and all of these are influenced by the climate, geology and geography. So although these regions are in the same country, their cooking style is completely different.

In England we would normally just use the phrase regional cooking as the climate is not a great variant – except in the case of Kent. The county is almost all coastline stretching from the Thames Estuary all the way round to the English Channel. The northern coast is largely historic salt marsh.

This makes for good for grazing, especially for sheep, and historically it meant salt could be made here. The flooding of the marshes would provide an opportunity to trap water in sluices and then evaporate the water by boiling. In the case of Seasalter, the proximity of the woodlands, or Blean, meant there was an energy supply and the Domesday Book notes that people had the right to chop down two trees a year for this purpose. Being surrounded by sea also affects the climate as it moderates extremes of temperature. One consideration is the location of Kent within the UK. The prevailing weather systems come across the Atlantic from west to east which means that rain tends to fall more in the west where it first hits land and results in a drier climate in eastern counties of the UK. This is known as a rain shadow.

Kent also gets more sunshine and higher temperatures than most areas of the country. This helps to explain why it grows soft fruit, such as strawberries, cherries and others so successfully. Inland is the Weald of Kent, where the lush green pasture that produces milk and cream of the highest quality. This means the butter and cheese is potentially as good as any from Normandy or the Charentes.

Another interesting area is the Isle of Thanet, the easterly most point of Kent. It is important to note that the largest greenhouse complex in Europe, Thanet Earth, is located here because the light is brighter than in any other place in the UK, and it's because light is critical to the growing of tomatoes and peppers that this was the place chosen to house the development. Another element of the county's unique *terroir* is the amount of game that is found, due to the diverse habitats of the marshlands and Weald.

On a micro scale, the small region that I am principally concerned with, Seasalter, has its own defining characteristics. The estuary coast has some of the best oyster beds in the world, and the beaches provide bladderwrack, gutweed, sea lettuce, sea buckthorn and sea vegetables that have never been properly exploited in British food. The salt from the marshes also make it possible to preserve meat or fish using the traditional methods that helped people to survive the lean days of winter.

If you put all of these factors together then Kent has so many high quality ingredients that are a result of its geography, geology, climate and history that there is no doubt we can call it a *terroir*.

River Thames

• Sittingbourne

• Teynham

TO LONDON

• Otterden Place

• Challo

• Betherdsen

• ASHFOR

N

W   E

S

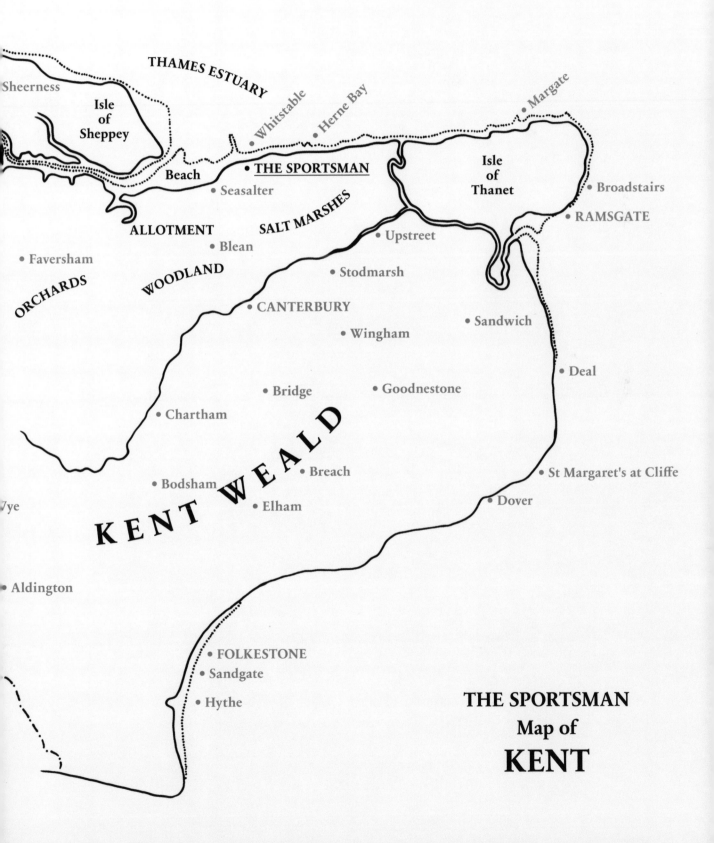

THE NORTH SEA

THAMES ESTUARY

Sheerness

Isle
of
Sheppey

Whitstable

Herne Bay

Margate

Beach

• THE SPORTSMAN

• Seasalter

Isle
of
Thanet

• Broadstairs

ALLOTMENT

SALT MARSHES

RAMSGATE

• Blean

• Upstreet

WOODLAND

• Faversham

ORCHARDS

• Stodmarsh

• CANTERBURY

• Sandwich

• Wingham

• Deal

• Bridge

• Goodnestone

• Chartham

KENT WEALD

• Breach

• St Margaret's at Cliffe

• Bodsham

• Dover

Wye

• Elham

• Aldington

• FOLKESTONE

• Sandgate

• Hythe

THE SPORTSMAN
Map of
KENT

SOUTH SWALE NATURE RESERVE

THIS LAND IS A NATURE RESERVE MANAGED
BY THE KENT TRUST FOR NATURE CON-
SERVATION AND ACQUIRED WITH THE
ASSISTANCE OF THE NOEL C. FULLER
TRUST FUND.

A Brief History of Seasalter

In the early days of The Sportsman, when I started to make my own salt and cure hams, researching age-old techniques, I happened to bump into an old friend of mine in a café in Whitstable, Tim, who is an archeologist. I was telling him about how the pub was going, and my experiments; coincidentally, he had just written a paper entitled 'Seasalter, Swine and Seafood', all about the history of the area and its long-held status as the Canterbury Cathedral 'larder'. I wrote a list of all the things that grew within a few miles of the pub, and this ended up informing the tasting menu. This essay, written by Tim, shows how this chance meeting helped focus my style of cooking.

Stephen Harris

The Sportsman is located on the north Kent coast, between the towns of Whitstable and Faversham, in a corner of South East England. To the south lies a wooded upland called the Blean, but The Sportsman itself is surrounded by the salt and 'sweet' (fresh-water) marshes that characterise the rather strange Borough of Seasalter. Part of Seasalter's mystery arises from its geographic location, where drifts of sea mist alternate with extraordinary views across marshes, reed beds and rolling hills, but a hidden secret lies in its rich culinary tradition, a tradition extending deep into recorded history and beyond.

As its implies, Seasalter's culinary history is inextricably linked with the production of salt (the name derives from the Old English *sae-sealt-aern*, meaning 'the sea salt house'). Also remarkable, however, is the fact that Seasalter was designated a borough, because the ancient boroughs were usually created by early Anglo-Saxon kings around important towns, and this could hardly have been the case for the tiny and dispersed hamlets of rural Seasalter.

In 1066 William of Normandy famously conquered England. He then commissioned the Domesday Book, effectively a survey to find out exactly what he had conquered, but at the same time he demanded another survey, called Domesday Monachorum, to find out what important lands and other possessions were held by the archbishops of Canterbury. Amongst these was the Borough of Seasalter, which earned the terse statement 'assigned to the support of the archbishop's kitchen'. The Domesday Book itself confirms this with the following:

'In Borowart lath [a lath is an Anglo-Saxon sub-division of a county], there lies a small borough named Sesaltre, which properly belongs to the kitchen of the archbishop. One named Blize held it of the monks. In demesne there is one carucate, and forty-eight borderers with one carucate. There is a church and eight fisheries, with a rent of twenty-five shillings. Wood for the pannage [pasture] of ten hogs. In the time of king Edward the Confessor, and afterwards, it was worth twenty-five shillings, and now one hundred shillings.' Fisheries and hogs emerge here from the fog of archaic Norman terminology but, strangely, no mention is made of salt. This is because the historic Borough of Seasalter extended a considerable distance eastwards into what is now Whitstable. The ancient border between the borough of Seasalter and Whitstable was – and is – complicated and unclear. However, Whitstable (called 'Nortone' in the Domesday Book) is described as having seven salt houses, making it the third-richest salt-producing centre in Kent, and it is safe to assume that the salt houses referred to were actually in Seasalter.

The importance of salt cannot be overstated; it was and is essential to sustaining human life but also, before the age of refrigeration, it had enormous value as a means of preserving meat and fish. Salt was important enough to be used as a measure of value and as currency (sayings like 'worth his salt' are commonplace, and the word 'salary' derives from the Latin *salarius*, meaning 'salt money'). Just as importantly, large quantities of salt were required to maintain herds of domesticated animals that could not forage for it independently. For example, the salt requirement of a horse is up to five times greater than that of a human being, that of a cow up to ten times greater. With this in mind, it begins to seem reasonable that Seasalter was designated a borough; it clearly represented a great source of wealth.

'Wood for the pannage [pasture] of ten hogs' is a telling phrase in the Domesday extract quoted previously because pigs, or swine, as they were more commonly called, represented a critically important part of the traditional diet of the inhabitants of this remote and backward area, where the stiff and clay-heavy soil did not allow for productive agriculture. Compensation was to be found in the upland woods of the Blean, which provided fuel but also provided convenient pannage for pigs. The Blean was described in a very early document dated 724 (before the establishment of England, when Kent was still an independent kingdom) as a *pascum porcorum* ('pig pasture'). They said pigs belonging to the nuns of Thanet Minster, at a time when Thanet was still an island lying some twelve miles to the east. Clearly long-distance swine herding was a requirement of the times.

The use and importance of the Blean for swine grazing during the Anglo-Saxon period has had a lasting effect on the area's place-names. The term 'den' or 'dene' in a place-name derives from the Anglo-Saxon *denn*, meaning 'woodland swine pasture', and a great many wood names in the Blean contain this element, examples being Bishopsden Wood, Thornden Wood, Bossenden Wood, Denstroude Wood and Denstead Wood. This is because swine remained a very important food source throughout the Anglo-Saxon and medieval periods. Pigs produce larger litters, and being omnivorous, are easier to feed than animals with a more specialised diet. Moreover, virtually all of the pig can be cooked and eaten, from trotter to snout, although the latter clearly requires some culinary imagination. It was customary to slaughter all but the breeding stock in the autumn, and to preserve the meat by salting (salt clearly being readily available) in order to provide the supply of fat and protein required during the winter. Pigs were also important because pasture rights in the area, including rights of pannage, depended on the lord of the estate receiving payment of either one swine a year or one swine in ten, whichever was the greater. But for many living in the Seasalter area, kind was more likely to be salt or fish.

Seasalter, of course, lies next to the sea, and this provided an enormous amount of food in the form of fish and shellfish, with the oysters for which Whitstable is still famous making up a large proportion of the latter. Oysters were caught by members of the local oyster companies, three of which still operate in the Faversham, Seasalter and Whitstable area. Extraordinarily, these companies appear to have originated from semi-independent medieval fishermen operating with a high degree of freedom, partly immune from the tight feudal constraints that operated elsewhere. The members of the Company or Fraternity of Free Fishermen, for example, were technically tenants of Faversham Abbey but worked the oyster fishery from about 1205 as freemen, not as feudal vassals.

The local fishermen and the infamous 'fishwives' also acted with a high degree of independence. Fish were caught in nets but also in large, usually triangular fish traps made of upright wooden posts and stakes set in the inter-tidal area and designed to trap the fish in the seaward-pointing apex of the triangle as the tide went out. The archeological evidence suggests that fish, mussels, whelks and oysters were eaten in large amounts in many dwellings, whether humble or grand, on the coast in and around Seasalter, but much was also transported to the fish market in Canterbury (paradoxically known as Whitstable Market) carried there in baskets by the fishwives, a round-trip of twelve miles. In the mid-fourteenth century, when the much-hated Canterbury tax collector tried, inadvisably, to extract documented payments from them, they gave him a good beating.

The granting of an entire borough to the kitchens of Canterbury Cathedral, then the most eminent monastic institution in England, indicates just how important Seasalter was during the Early Norman period, but as we've already seen, the gastronomic status of the area was well established, even before the Norman Conquest. In 786, exactly three hundred years before the Domesday Book was completed, another Anglo-Saxon document refers to the area as *sealterna steallas thear bi uban et in Blean uuidiung thaer to*, this meaning 'the saltwork sheds to the north and their associated woodland in Blean'. Another charter, issued in the following year, refers to a permission to collect *silvam afundantur ad coquendam sal*, meaning 'enough wood to evaporate, literally to cook salt'. Indeed, access to the Blean was considered important enough in 863 to warrant control by a later king, who designated it a royal wood and king's common. Predictably, then as now, the value of an area as a resource for food and fuel could be gauged by the interest taken in it by those in power.

Salt production in Seasalter has been proven in recent years to predate the well-documented Anglo-Saxon industry by several thousand years. Many small, porous coarse-ware clay vessels were used to store and transport salt during the later Bronze Age and throughout the Iron Age, have been found in in the area, including on the Seasalter foreshore, which was still dry land during those periods.

So, in Seasalter, the rich salt-water fisheries and good pasture for cattle, sheep and pigs, combined with the availability of shellfish and thriving salt industry, represented a most valuable resource, with the borough effectively being the principal supplier for the kitchens of Canterbury Cathedral, some five miles to the southeast. And it should be noted here that, while church institutions such as Canterbury Cathedral were extremely powerful, owned large estates and employed large numbers of people, they were also largely monastic organisations. It is not known how many monks lived in the cathedral's monastic complex but its sheer size suggests there were many hundreds, requiring very well stocked larders and busy kitchens (the remains of which can still be seen in the cathedral grounds). It should also be mentioned that, in later medieval times, monks, having taken vows of obedience, chastity and poverty, eventually, gained notoriety for their great appetites and love of good food. Monkshill Farm, near Faversham, supplied

The Sportsman with produce of exceptional quality, incredibly, until its closure in 2015, having been originally founded to meet just those appetites. No-one knows exactly when, but the clue lies in the name of the farm, and certainly predated Henry VIII's dissolution of the monastery of Canterbury Cathedral.

Anyone approaching The Sportsman from Faversham to the west, across the Graveney Marshes, will notice two sets of earthworks, one consisting of grass-covered humps punctuating the marshland flats to the south, the other a long linear bank lying between the Seasalter Road and the Cleve Marshes to the north. Both tell the informed observer much about history of the area. The humps are the remains of Anglo-Saxon and medieval salterns (saltworks), with the two excavated so far dating from the late twelfth- or thirteenth-century date. The salt was extracted by boiling brine already concentrated by exposure to the sun (actually a similar method to that now employed to meet the salt requirements of The Sportsman). The salt was then transported over rough tracks, many of which survive as rights of way and are still known as salt ways, with much of the salt not required by the monks being sold at the salt market (called Salt Hill) in Canterbury.

Salt production on this small scale within or on the margins of the salt marshes continued until 1325, when a massively destructive flood, effectively a tsunami, swamped the area, which was then deemed to be at risk of permanent inundation. In response, Canterbury Cathedral commissioned the construction of an earth-sea defence, now visible as the large-built bank partly skirting Seasalter Road. The construction of the bank marked the end of the salterns, which lay south of the road and so were now separated from the areas where salt marsh could form and briny water be collected for boiling. However, further to the east, local salt production continued using large 'inned' areas where sea water was collected and allowed to evaporate to make concentrated brine. At the end of the eighteenth century a Mr (later Alderman) Bunce was still producing and selling 'marine boiled salt'.

History, therefore, tells us what people in the area ate for well over a thousand years before the Industrial Revolution nearly destroyed what was a unique food culture rooted in the local terrain and its long-term management. We know that fish and seafood, along with pork, lamb, beef and, most important of all, salt, comprised the basis for this culture, and The Sportsman has for many years now been engaged in the process of discovering how all these ingredients (and, of course, many more) can be prepared and combined in ways that revive and maintain the ancient local culinary tradition, and point to new and imaginative ways of interpreting it.

Tim Allen

From 'No Future' to No Sommeliers

I have heard some people say they see colours when they cook, and that this is how they make sense of food. I don't know how that works but I can understand, as I see food and music as analogous.

When I am finishing a sauce or soup, I can't help thinking like I would if I had a graphic equaliser and was balancing something in a song. The treble is like acidity, so if I need a bit more I add a few drops of lemon or lime juice, or cider vinegar. The idea is not to be able to taste the lemon, but to stimulate the sides of the mouth and create an illusion that the whole of the mouth is filled. It is a bit like those old buttons on stereos marked 'wide' – press the button and the sound appeared to spread out and seem bigger.

I see salt as bass, which is easy to adjust, although I always check how new chefs season their dishes. If they are using Maldon or our homemade salt, both of which come in flakes, I make sure they rub it between their fingers to break it down a bit; I get strange looks when I ask young chefs to show me how they season, but it is so fundamental that it should be discussed.

The mid-range is umami, and it is true that if you don't have a strong middle, in music or food, then you will struggle to 'finish' with adjustments to seasoning. The mid-range gives a dish depth and should be there when the cooking is done – it can be solved by adjusting the recipe to add an umami element, such as Parmesan or even ketchup, which increases the savouriness. In winemaking the French have a word, *matière*, which translates as 'material' or 'stuff', and this seems to be in the mid-range. If you are tasting a dish to finish the seasoning and it lacks 'middle', then you probably haven't followed the stages properly, from reduction, deglazing and other methods that help to develop flavour. To use another musical term, these processes create a kind of compression, because they focus and concentrate flavour.

Without wishing to torture this extended analogy, I also see the rise of the gastropub in musical terms. When I was looking for a site for my restaurant, before finding The Sportsman, I read an article in the trade press that said that it costs £1 million to open a Michelin-starred restaurant. What they meant was a 'posh' restaurant, as the two were seen as the same – no relaxed restaurant had stars back then, not even the River Café or St.John.

This reminded me of the mid-seventies, when to form a band would cost a fortune, because you needed twenty-piece drum kit – complete with a gong – as well as banks of keyboards, synthesisers and emulators. And not forgetting those huge four-by-four cabinets, to make sure the lead guitar made your ears bleed. Then the music required a degree from the Royal College to play, as you offered up your interpretation of a Mussorgsky piece.

The whole music industry had become bloated and needed to be taken down a peg or two. That is why punk was so refreshing in 1976. It gave people the confidence to form bands with limited equipment but lots of talent. It should be said, of course, that there was also a load of rubbish – which is where the image of punk came from – but the important thing was that it was a revolution from the bottom up.

I thought of this as I plotted a way of opening my own place. All I needed was a building with four walls, a roof and a kitchen; the rest of the trappings felt unnecessary.

I didn't like the idea of a restaurant floor packed with staff who had just the one job, like handing out the cutlery; a waiter who was only there to sneer at your choice of wine and then hide it from you on the other side of the room. In such places, I could sometimes feel the eyes of all the floor staff burning into the back of my head as they waited for me to finish what I was eating. Of course in most restaurants, the floor staff were professional, but in others, there was neither the skill nor numbers of trained staff to execute this style of service. This meant that you often had a young, poorly trained waiter carrying out a function that he clearly didn't understand. Being well brought up, I would often spend the meal trying to help make his evening run smoother.

I realised we would have to find a different way to serve the food, and it was a visit to the Walnut Tree in Abergavenny that gave me the answer. The front-of-house staff were just bright, intelligent people from the town who carried out their function as if it were a busy café: fast, friendly and efficient with no pretence, formality or uniforms. I had gone from 'No Future' to 'No Sommeliers' in twenty years.

I was beginning to like this idea of a jumble sale Michelin-starred restaurant. It divided people, and some really didn't like it. They liked the tablecloths, crockery and sommeliers because these things told them they were in a good restaurant. This was just plain snobbery and needed to be challenged. Would these people recognise that the food was as good or better than many top restaurants without these signifiers? Either way, I wanted to find out.

DIARY OF

Stephen Harris

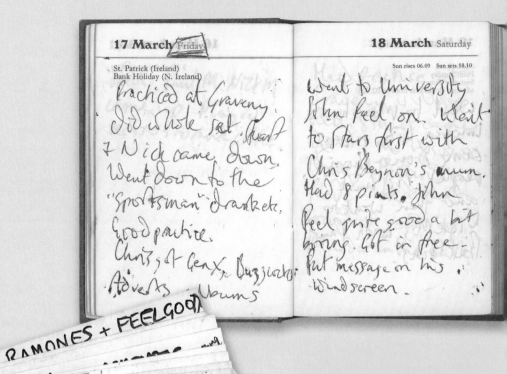

17 March Friday

St. Patrick (Ireland)
Bank Holiday (N. Ireland)

Practiced at Graveny
did whole set. Stuart
7 Nick came down.
Went down to the
"Sportsman" drank etc.
Good practice.
Chris, at Geax, Buzzcocks
Adverts   Nouns

18 March Saturday

Sun rises 06.09   Sun sets 18.10

Went to University
John feel on. Went
to stars first with
Chris Beynon's mum.
Had 8 pints. John
feel quite good a bit
lying. Got in free.
Put message on his
windscreen.

Here are a few old photos
which I still have of the group.
The singer is Ben Chalkes and
the other guitarist is Nick Appleton.
We were all at school together.

Invoice   Date 01-12-99   14

RSDC - Monkshill farm

free Range Eggs

V.A.T. Regd. No.

Sportsman P.H.

Description	£	P
09-11-99	4 doz	
19-11-99	4 doz	
27-11-99	4 doz	
	12 doz @ £1-30/doz	

Terms   % V.A.T.

TOTAL £15-60

Date Posted

The diary shows our first bookings. We had forgotten to buy a diary and so I grabbed my own to write the names in. We were quite busy after just a few weeks.

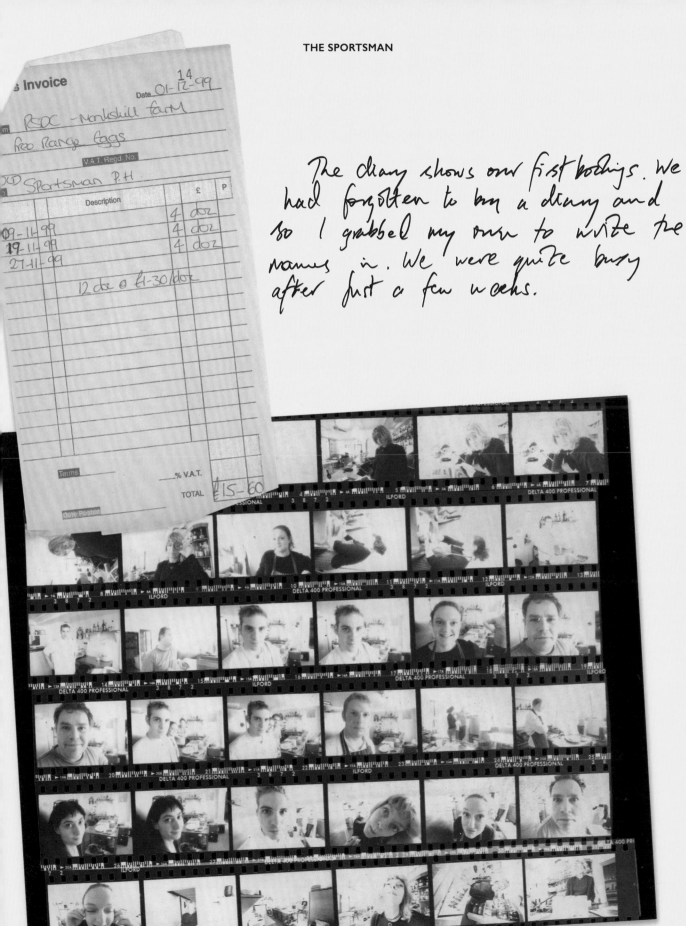

*This our first Christmas menu.
Looks like a bargain at £15/head.*

Christmas at the Sportsman

**Watercress Soup
(with or without Oysters)**

**Salmon, marinated in vodka, lemon & lime,
with lumpfish roe and sour cream**

**Anti-Pasti - a mixed plate of salami, serrano ham
olives, peppers, salt cod etc.**

**Roast Breast of Duck, Roast Potatoes,
Savoy Cabbage, Cranberry and Chilli Gravy**

**Roast Cod with Mash, Braised Gem Lettuce,
Roast Tomato Sauce and Tapenade**

**Roast Field Mushrooms, Stuffed with Sour Cream and
Guacamole of Peas, Mash, Savoy Cabbage
and Smoked Chilli Sauce**

**Italian Christmas Cake Bread
and Butter Pudding
or**

Hot Chocolate Mousse with Clemantine Granita

£15.00 per head

Service not included - all tips go to staff

For bookings and enquiries please call 01227 273370

Northern Rhone Wine Supper at The Sportsman

Condrieu Les Terrasses du Palat 2003, Francois Villard
Scallop Roe Crisps and Petit Lucques Olives

Saint Joseph Mairlant 2004, Francois Villard
Crab Risotto

Crozes Hermitage Cuvee Gaby 2004, Domaine Du Colombier
Saint Joseph Les Pierres 2001, Earl Pierre Gaillard
Slow Baked Organic Salmon Fillet with an Avruga Caviar

Côte Rôtie 2003, Earl Pierre Gaillard
Hermitage 2000, Tardieu-Laurent (Negociants Lourmarin)
Roast Rack and Braised Shoulder of Monkshill Farm Lamb

Cornas Les Eygats 2000, Domaine Courbis
Cornas 1997, Alain Voge
Unpasteurized Cheeses

Condrieu Fleurs D'Automne 2001, Earl Pierre Gaillard
Choice of Pudding

Monsieur, Madam

Nous avons un restaurant en Angleterre, et nous voudrions acheter des marchandises au entrepôt 'Metro' à Calais, sans T.V.A. Veuillez trouver ci-joint notre certificat de T.V.A, et aussi la preuve que nous sommes les propriétaires d'un restaurant. Nous arriverons à Calais le 7 décembre (mardi). Je vous saurais gré de bien vouloir assurer que la carte d'acheteur et les documents sont prêt.

Je vous prie d'agréer l'expression de mes sentiments distingués,

Monsieur / Madam,

Nous avons un restaurant en Angleterre, et nous voudrions acheter des marchandises au entrepôt 'Metro' à Calais, sans T.V.A. Veuillez trouver ci-joint notre certificat de T.V.A, et aussi la preuve que nous sommes les propriétaires d'un restaurant. Nous arriverons à Calais le 7 décembre (mardi). Je vous saurais gré de bien vouloir assurer que la carte d'acheteur et les documents sont prêt.

Je vous prie d'agréer l'expression de mes sentiments distingués

Philip + Stephen Harris

WOT! NO

V.

aussi

Stott - Benham
model GHR 5·4B MG
Serial No. - 1498
B.T.U. - 99,000

TONY
0973 360504

CANTERBURY
SHEET METAL.

SPORTSMAN

Music

make good atmosphere tapes
By the Sea - Suede
English Rose - Jam
Song to Siren - This mortal coil
Local Boch - Space Raiders
Lazy - Suede

1914
MONIES 5kg 10×40

£500 FOR STOKE   £10 LISA
£40   FRANCS
119.45   STOKE
160·56   WHITE WORLD
20·01   PETROL
30·72   PETROL
3·45   MURP
125·81
118·92   125·81
                32·31   GOOSE
6·89 short   11·88 FOOD FOR
                       MONDAY
                37·89 B+Q

                43·73
                10·00 PETROL
                33·73

0151 870 9575

The Sportsman

Faversham Road, Seasalter,
Whitstable, Kent CT5 4BP.
Telephone: 01227 273370.

'Matchless'

The Sportsman

Here is an old tasting menu from
when we were working on the design.
It was Dan's birthday.

The Sportsman

Oysters and chorizo, pickled herring and soda bread, homemade
unpasteurized butter and Seasalter seasalt

Wood pigeon, native oyster and miso broth

18 month salt cured Seasalter ham

Braised brill fillet with an avruga caviar sauce and deep fried oyster

Roast rump of Seasalter marsh lamb with
chestnut and root vegetable confit

Rhubarb sorbet and burnt cream

Chocolate soufflé

Apple parfait, hazelnuts and wild blackberry sorbet

Wednesday 1st November

HAPPY BIRTHDAY DANNO!

Here are some pictures of the pizzas we did at lunchtime in the very early days. Opposite is part of our original proposal to Shepherd Neame, the brewers who own the building.

OYSTER + CHORIZO
OYSTER, APPLE, HAM
ANGELS ON HORSEBACK
BAKED OYSTER, GRANITA SEAWEED
LANGOUSTINE RAW
CRAB, CARROT, HOLLANDAISE
LOBSTER ? SEAWEED +
         DRIED MACKEREL
(SHELLFISH SOUP)
HALIBUT + AVRUGA SAUCE
BAKED COD + APPLE BALSAMIC
MERINGUE ICE CREAM + SEA
         BUCKTHORN
HOT CHOCOLATE MOUSSE

OYSTERS - ROCK
     + NATIVE X 2 courses
LANGOUSTINE - FOR
         2 courses
LOBSTER - FOR ONE
         COURSE
CRAB - enough for
     one course
Carrots
AVRUGA CAVIARE
HALIBUT
COD
WALNUT OIL
CELERY
APPLES - G. SMITH
CREME FRAICHE 2 litres
2 BUNCHES PARSLEY
CHESTNUTS
CHOCOLATE

Opportunities:

① Land to grow own produce eg herbs + veg.

② Space → suitable to families w. children

③ Build up reputation as a location pub/restaurant - Change the nature of the trade.

④ Provide a pub venue for 25-50 age range. *highquality* restaurant

⑤ His van *currently* under achieving site; which could become a focal as venue for good local produce + trade.

THREATS:

① Seasonality.

② Changing the nature of a pub → local opinion?

Strengths   Is on Official "Saxon Walk" !

① location → destination pub/walks   Parking.
② Size → sea/atmosphere   Al fresco.
        → suppliers → local produce

        → flexibility + expansion of current level of business.

③ Caravan Park ?   → steady / reliable income.
                     (valuable background income).

④ ~~Large kitchen~~ → plenty of storage.

④ Whitstable is expriencing media interest / food (will cause locals to move further afield?) boom.

WEAKNESSES:

① Location → strongly seasonal

② Reputation → seen as locals as run down
Not currently known as a good food venue.   + used by holiday makers.

③ Interior decoration requires considerable improvement.

④ It may take longer time to build up a reputation as a good food venue due to it's location. Not able to rely on local trade as such.

⑤ Drink + Driving

Notes   63

           GOOD SERVICE   The Sportsman 9.11.99

- SAY HELLO AS SOON AS SOMEONE   1 sack banana shallots   550
  COMES IN   1 box leeks   380
                                  1 sack Maris Piper   * 300
- DON'T AVOID PEOPLES EYE, ACKNOWLEDGE 1 flat parsley   80
                                  4 celery   180
- SOMETHING MUST ARRIVE QUICKLY, 1 box carrots   3-20
  OLIVES, BREAD, DRINK   1 string garlic (3 nets £3.00) 3-50
                                  5lb green beans (box)   7-50
- CLEAR TABLES QUICKLY BUT NOT   1 tarragon   80
  HOVERING   15 little gem   3-30
                                  20 lemons   3-00
- BILL READY QUICKLY   1 box watercress   6-00
                                  1 box v ripe tomatoes 5-50
                                  1 chives   80
                                  5 spring onion   2-25
                                  5 savoy   1-81
                                  1 sage   80
                                  4 oz fresh red chillies 33
                                  2lb cavolo nero or 2lb spinach 2-90
                                  ROCKET
                                                        56.89

The Sportsman!

This is me with my Epiphone guitar which I bought for £65 in 1976.

Dan Flavell
Head Chef

I met Stephen at my first job in a restaurant kitchen twenty years ago; I was eighteen and in charge of washing up. It was a Mexican place in Canterbury called Café des Amis, and Stephen was a chef there – I was at art college in Canterbury at the time, so it was just a job that paid the bills. His passion was, and still is, a really attractive quality. I think partly I just hopped on board with it. Working together and living a couple of streets away from each other in Whitstable, we quickly became friends.

If I'm honest, I'm artistic, but I've never been particularly self-motivated, and that's probably why I responded so well to the kitchen environment – you don't have the opportunity to do very little. I decided to leave college and work in restaurants fairly swiftly. The decision was partly made for me as my then-girlfriend was pregnant, but looking back, I'd also fallen in love with the kitchen environment; it's so exciting and creative.

Stephen was much more driven than any other chef I'd met, someone who was never going to follow the crowd. He's the one who took me for my first Michelin-starred meal at Sandbank in Southend as soon as I started at The Sportsman. It was our way of learning techniques and how to replicate them in our kitchen, and it's something we've continued doing ever since.

I started six months after the pub opened, so I've built the place up with Stephen; it feels as much mine as it is his. We joke that he is the Mick Jagger of the operation. I'm the craftsman to his artist; it's why we work so well together. I suppose that was the problem with art college for me – I'm less of an abstract person, I work well with what's in front of me, and that's just what I do in the kitchens at The Sportsman. Although I'm here every day, I only sit down and eat in the restaurant about once a year. There's something surprising about eating the food you are tasting every day, to experience it in the way our customers do. I'm proud that the food we cook is accessible to everyone.

I remember the first time I went to The Sportsman, it was so grotty and run down. I'm from the area, but I had no idea it existed, it felt like the middle of nowhere. Sixteen years on, and it's the centre of my world. What I love about the pub is that it's constantly evolving. Slowly, yes, but it's always changing.

The allotment will be our next big challenge, and I'm so excited to see what will grow well – Stephen is keen on getting peas to work, and broad beans. We're experimenting with planting the same crops in different places too, so we can get the very best results, even if it takes a little time to work it all out and get started properly. We're not rushing ahead, but we are determinedly moving forward.

Shelley Barnfather
Front of House

I was a teaching assistant at Whitstable community college, and I met Stephen when we were both working at the Oyster Company in the mid-nineties. I'd actually gotten to know his brother Phil first, as he ran the chess club at the school, and through him I started working part time at The Sportsman in the summer holidays. Eventually, I stopped teaching and worked full time as front of house – Phil can be very persuasive.

Even back when Stephen, Dan and I were at the Oyster Company, I could tell Stephen had a different approach to cooking. I was born in New Zealand and grew up on an organic dairy farm with orchards, gardens and meadows. I suppose what my parents were doing was ground-breaking at that time, and it's most likely why I was drawn to Stephen's style of cooking. Twenty years ago, it was rare for chefs to go to farms and work closely with them to build relationships, even if it's commonplace now.

My kids have been brought up on the food at The Sportsman, on Stephen's cooking. Because of the tough lifestyle, I told them, 'never become chefs' – but, as with a lot of my friends who work in the restaurant and catering industry, most of their children often do end up working in it as well. My daughter lives in New York and works in fashion, but my sons both work in kitchens now, having started washing up in The Sportsman from when they were fourteen. At the moment, my oldest, who is thirty, is a head chef at a restaurant in Canterbury, and my youngest works at The Sportsman. Whitstable is kind of a funny town for that too, I think; there's a core of families whose grandparents are still walking up and down the high street, and the traditions continue.

We get such a mix of people here, from A-listers to young couples coming to celebrate their anniversary, and we often deal with a lot of big personalities, but there's one rule: everyone is as important as everyone else. I don't have a computerised system or a detailed reservation list, far from it – I just talk to people to find out a bit more about what they like. You can walk in with a baby, a big family or as a solo walker just in off the beach, but I love serving tables of chefs – you can always tell, because they pick up their plates to smell the food before eating it.

If there was a camera on the wall I'm sure it'd make for funny viewing. We have arguments, and good shifts and bad shifts, but that's because we're so close knit.

Yes, it's a restaurant, but to me, it also feels like we're inviting people into The Sportsman. If it's not what people want, then we don't change to suit; the pub is like our home in many ways. Some places try to be everything to everybody, we just don't.

It's wonderful driving out here to work, coming from an urban area. The Sportsman is rural, but I wouldn't say it's too remote. I like to watch people looking out at the marshes when they visit, standing absolutely still. It's not chocolate-box pretty, I know, but it has a magic – and I never have, and never will, feel bored when I see it.

Emma Read
Front of House

I'd worked in other restaurants as a teenager, to get some pocket money together for travelling, but my first career choice was journalism. I worked for the local paper, *The Whitstable Times*, but I realised that actually I didn't like the hard-nosed hack bit. My friend Daisy worked at The Sportsman when it first opened, so that's how I got a job there. I started in the kitchen, washing up and doing a bit of veg prep while I was at university in Canterbury. I'd cycle on my mum's old bike out to Seasalter to get to work. Shortly afterwards, I started to work as front of house, taking over from Stephen's sister when she left to set up another restaurant, co-managing with Shelley. That was in 2003, and I've worked at the pub ever since.

I actually went to The Sportsman for my 21st birthday. My grandmother was a character, and she wrote a letter to them to make a reservation – I think she's the only person that's ever booked that way. Steve still has the letter. In fact, it wasn't long after that that I started working there. I remember he created a special dish for me that evening – I joke that it was called 'sea bass à la Emma'. I can still remember how amazing it tasted: steamed wild bass with crab and a tomato and olive oil dressing.

Growing up in Whitstable, though, I'd been to the pub in its previous incarnation. My dad used to take us for a drive to weird and wonderful places at the weekend when I was a kid, treating us to some crisps and a drink at a pub on the way home. Back then, The Sportsman was one of those kinds of places; I remember that it was very dark, and the car park just stank of horrible old chip fat.

Stephen and I became friends, and saw each other socially a lot, then our relationship just developed from there. We kept it quiet for a bit at first, but we've been together for fourteen years now. Stephen and I have always had a lot of similar interests – we like to travel a lot together, eating at restaurants around the world. I decided to take some time out from the restaurant, and then had our son, Stanley. He's four now, almost five. We don't live at the pub, but we always stay there on the weekends. As we both work there, we feel it's healthy to have a bit of space from it as well. But saying that, we want Stan to grow up here. He always has his Sunday lunch at the pub, sitting upstairs. Normally it's fish with beurre blanc and mash. I'd say that's his favourite, apart from strawberry ice cream, of course.

I think what makes The Sportsman special is the shared attitude. Steve's an old punk, so the ethos has always been 'why not?' And when I think about it, no-one who works here went straight into this kind of job – no-one was following a set path to work in the restaurant business, they all came to it late. I guess that's part of the sense of rebellion. There's such a sense of opportunity, a feeling that you could achieve anything. The Sportsman always feels like it's going somewhere, there's just a momentum that's hard to describe.

Sarah Kay
Pastry Chef

I started as a washer upper at The Sportsman when I was 15. I should really have been studying, but the kitchen environment was much more fun. I grew up in Whitstable, and a lot of the kids in the area worked at the pub, so it was a really sociable thing, too. In actual fact, I didn't really want to leave the washing up for a section, but I got bullied into it, first into veg prep, and then starters, and finally pastry. I suppose it was quite daunting to progress in an environment where I was a seventeen-year-old girl working with grown men, but once I started to move forwards, I just wanted to keep going.

I think I ended up in the pastry section because I have a good eye for what looks pretty. I love gardening – that's my other passion – and when it was quieter, I used to look after the garden at The Sportsman as well as my own allotment. I think also the time and space you get from prepping in advance on the pastry section is why I like it so much. When you're working on the stove, it can be quite monotonous, but with pastry, you're doing a little bit of everything. My favourite dessert on the menu is probably the elderflower posset and fritter. It just symbolises the start of summer – I love the fragrance of it. It's simple but stunning, a really nice, clean flavour.

I worked somewhere else briefly – at an accountants, as I thought I should see what a 'proper' job was like – but I remember coming home in tears one day, and Steve said if I came back, he'd give me my own section. That was when I worked on starters, and I haven't looked back.

I've worked here over half my life, and Dan and I have been together for ten years. We've always worked together, so I can't imagine it any other way. It's an antisocial lifestyle, I think if we didn't work at the same place, or at least in the same industry, then we would hardly see each other.

I think what sets The Sportsman apart is that everyone cares so much about what they do. You immediately notice if a chef comes along and doesn't care enough. They stick out like a sore thumb. And if there's a complaint from a customer – not that it happens very often – then we take it to heart.

In general, people don't tend to leave once they start working here, but if they do, then they seem to come back, I suppose a bit like I did. You see your colleagues more than you see your family. It's a funny relationship in catering – you can call each other all the names under the sun, but then you forget it as soon as the shift is over.

Stephen has taken us all over the world to eat at the best restaurants – Noma, L'Arpège, The Ledbury, The Fat Duck – he puts a lot in to get a lot out. I think the place that influenced my cooking the most, though, was L'Arpège. I have an allotment, and Alain Passard cooks with so many vegetables. It was incredible to see what can be done with the finest but simplest ingredients. I think that's the beauty of The Sportsman, too.

Total Cooking

I have always loved the idea of new concepts being introduced into certain fields that subsequently change the way they are studied and perceived.

Take the Dutch philosophy of 'Total Football'. Introduced in the seventies, it threw away the coaching manual whereby players had rigid positions and formations that often meant they were not free to pursue opportunities on the pitch. Instead, the players would be free to go anywhere and trust that their teammates would ensure that their position was covered. This meant that a player happily thinking that he had an easy day playing up against René van de Kerkhof could suddenly find himself confronted by Johan Cruyff. By rejecting traditional formations and rules 'total football' changed the way the game was played – even if it didn't win them the World Cup – and has now been absorbed into the mainstream, despite being revolutionary at the time. Dan and I used to joke about working in a similar manner. We were the only two chefs in the early days, and so we would go to any section, depending on which one of us was available.

When I was studying history at King's College, London, I realised that a group of early-twentieth-century historians from France, called the Annalists, followed a comparable philosophy. They questioned the idea that the lives of old kings, queens and great men determined what was recorded in history, and instead chose to study anything that might throw new light on world events – this became known as 'Total History'. They looked at things like the price of grain and how it was related to specific moments in time; they would look at paintings of market scenes to observe the changing fashions of the middle class and the static fashions of the peasants. Again, it changed the way history was studied and written, and has since been absorbed into the mainstream.

In trying to explain what we do at The Sportsman I realise that we take a similar approach – when people ask what my style is, I can only think of calling it 'total cooking'. We are constantly questioning our processes and trying new ideas, because it might make our food taste better. In the end, nothing else matters but the taste of the food wesend out to customers.

I have never worked under a great chef, and so I have had to figure everything out for myself. As a result I don't allow myself the luxury of having a fixed stance on anything. I am always surprised that chefs take up strong positions about a subject when just keeping an open mind might lead to improvements in the food they serve. For example, some chefs will say they hate the raw food movement, but I look at what is happening and try to take the best from it. This has resulted in a lot of fresh new ideas coming onto our menu, such as pickled vegetables.

I will happily apply techniques and principles from any movement and incorporate them into our style of cooking. It is important to realise that the coming and going of trends, such as molecular gastronomy or 'New Nordic', is of course a little about vogue and fashion, but the ideas at their centre can be eternal. Molecular gastronomy gave us new techniques for the slow cooking of protein and understanding of flavour compounds that demonstrated how to create new combinations, and this remains invaluable to chefs. Similarly, 'New Nordic' made fermentation and much cleaner, brighter food more mainstream, and that has begun to filter down to home cooks.

This idea of 'Total Cooking' even encompasses the location of The Sportsman. The small details of its surrounding geology are important because the soil and rock affect the types of crops that can be grown – we have to be aware of the full picture to get the best out of what this area has to offer.

Another aspect of our 'Total Cooking' is the running of the business itself. I feel strongly about keeping the wealth generated by the pub within the local economy, exploring new ways of working with what we have that can change the way we are perceived. It makes no sense to buy ingredients from a long way away when we have great stuff on our doorstep. The area around the pub has farms that produce brilliant vegetables, meat and eggs, so why shop further afield?

For the same reason, I wanted to use local chefs. I always felt a bit disappointed when I would eat at great restaurants where chefs and waiting staff came from all over the world – I wanted to see what the locals could do. At first, it wasn't really a choice, as we couldn't offer 'live-in', but this soon became a policy point. I believe it's so important to look after our new chefs and put an arm around them until they feel at home. It's taken the restaurant industry a while to realise that you have to look after your chefs, and not work them into the ground.

So, in short, 'Total Cooking' is about using everything that is available to make your food better. History, geology, employment policy, an open-minded attitude in the kitchen and even the welfare of the people who are willing to come and work for you.

The Sea

The Kent Coast and North Sea

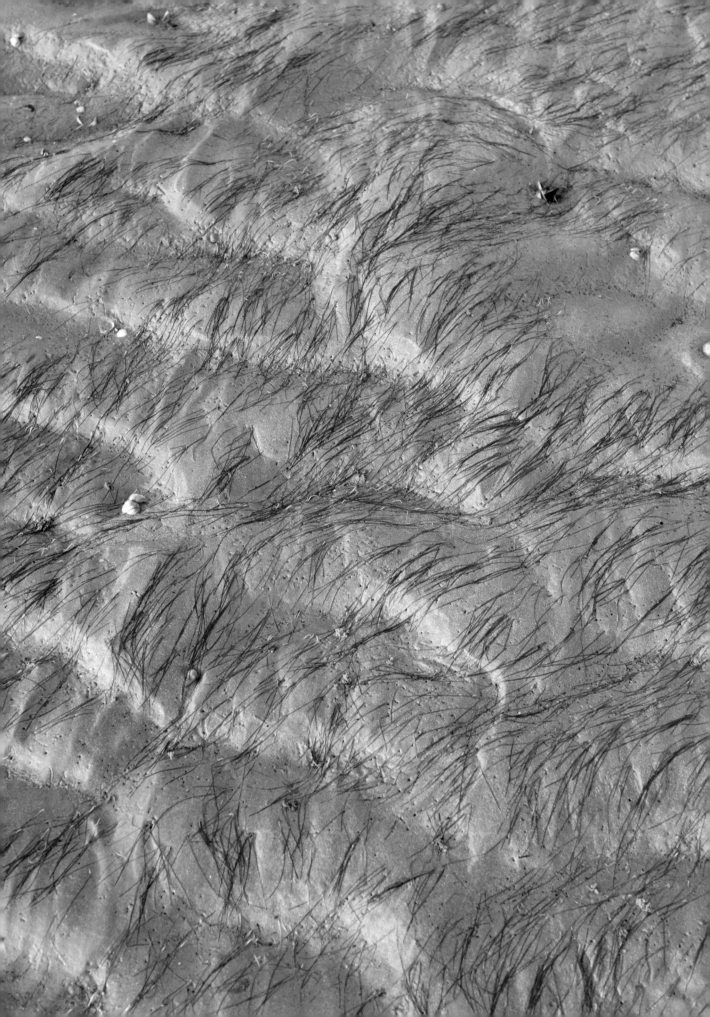

The Kent Coast and North Sea

I love to watch the fishing boats from Whitstable harbour disappear out to sea. I remember, back in the eighties when I was a teenager, seeing them head out at the end of long summer days from the vantage point of the beach by the Old Neptune pub. They have become less and less as the years pass, but I still admire the spirit that will take on the might of nature in a tiny boat with ramshackle equipment, the flags and buoys fluttering in the wind, a trail rippling behind the fishing boats as they head through the estuary and eventually out to sea. When looking into the history of it, it surprised me to find that the North Sea is scarcely more than 8,000 years old, and was formed as the ice melted from the last Ice Age. Before that, the countries surrounding it were joined together; for context, at this same point in time, the people of Egypt were well on the way to writing in hieroglyphs on papyrus and developing strong social and political structures. We think of our own land mass and social structures as so permanent, but we are all just passing through a fluid and ever-changing landscape.

In mainstream British food culture, Mediterranean influences have dominated since the 1960s, but in recent years, the countries surrounding the North Sea – the United Kingdom, Denmark, Belgium, the Netherlands and Norway – have regained some standing, the nuances of each place's cooking being recognised and celebrated as uniquely Northern European. As a result, it seems that Britain has developed new, stronger relationships with the great ingredients that come from and around this sea.

The coast has another gift to the chef – the seaweed and plants on the beach have proved to be remarkably important to the development of a local style of cooking. Gutweed, bladderwrack and sea lettuce, as well as succulents such as sandwort, samphire and purslane have become essential to our cooking. The seaweeds in particular are packed with umami; it seems strange that it has paid no part in English cooking until recently.

Although the ports of Whitstable and Ramsgate have provided us with much of our fish over the years, we get a lot from the company Griggs, who are based in Hythe. They drag their boats onto the beach and only go out for the day, which means the fish is caught, landed and delivered within a very short space of time. Turbot, brill, ray, cod, gurnard, sole and bass are the main fish we use, and they are undoubtedly the backbone of our cooking.

Rockpool

The inspiration for this dish came from a photograph I saw of a dish called 'Tidal Pool', created by David Kinch at his Manresa restaurant in California. The idea of similarly presenting the bay at Whitstable in a bowl was too good to miss. So I gathered together all the local sea vegetables and seafood I could find and served them in a bowl with a broth made from fish stock and seaweed. I suggest you use the seafood and sea vegetables listed below as a guide. These are the main items that I use, but you should use the best and freshest ingredients that are available.

Serves 6

Seaweed stock
· turbot or brill fish bones, roughly chopped
· 2 leeks, finely sliced
· 2 large celery stalks, finely chopped
· 1 large onion, finely chopped
· 1 fennel bulb, finely chopped
· 1 small bunch parsley, roughly chopped
· 1 star anise
· handful of dried bladderwrack (or use kombu)
· sea salt, to taste

Seafood
· 30 cockles, cooked, shelled and grit removed
· 6 native oysters
· 30 winkles
· 30 g/1 ¼ oz white crab meat [pp. 245]
· 1 ½ teaspoons Scallop Roe Powder [pp. 246]

Sea vegetables
· 30 sea purslane leaves
· 12 sea beet leaves
· 2 teaspoons Crystallised Seaweed Powder [pp. 245]
· 3 wild rose petals, shredded
· sprig of dried bladderwrack, to serve

First, prepare the seaweed stock. Combine all the ingredients, except for the bladderwrack and salt, in a large pan and add enough filtered water to cover. Bring to a boil, then lower the heat and simmer for 10 minutes. Turn off the heat and leave to infuse for 15 minutes.

Put the bladderwrack in a large bowl. Strain the seaweed stock into the bowl and leave to infuse for 2 hours. Strain through a J Cloth, then taste and adjust the seasoning if necessary.

Prepare the sea vegetables, as required. For example sea purslane and sea beet must be blanched, separately, to remove any bitterness.

Before serving, make sure that the seafood and sea vegetables are all at room temperature. Measure out 1 litre/34 fl oz (4 ¼ cups) of the seaweed stock and heat in a pan, then pour into a teapot with a sprig of dried bladderwrack and leave to infuse for 5 minutes.

While the stock is infusing, combine the seafood and vegetables, then divide among six attractive serving bowls. Take to the table, pour on the stock in front of your guests, and see the bowl come to life.

Seaweed butter

Sometimes everything just comes together. An idea seems to be perfect with all the loose ends tied up. I had such a moment during a shopping trip to St. Malo in Brittany. I was visiting Jean-Yves Bordier, the great French butter maker whose butter appears at the beginning of many great meals in France's top restaurants, and I was taken by his *beurre d'algues*, which is a butter flecked with locally picked green, brown and red seaweeds.

I had been making my own butter at The Sportsman for a while and it seemed obvious to me that I should attempt a version using the seaweed from my beach in Seasalter. I picked a load of sea lettuce and washed it many times to remove all of the sand, then I put it into my dehydrator for several hours at about 80°C/175°F until the whole kitchen smelt of the seaside. Once the seaweed was very dry I ground it up into small flakes.

I made a batch of my usual raw-cream butter and added some of the ground seaweed, along with some sea salt: the butter turned bright green and tasted sensational. It was moreish in the way things that are very umami tend to be. Something free that grows abundantly on the beach and which makes everything taste delicious seemed too good to be true. You'll find the recipe for this on pp.226.

Scallops
in seaweed butter

In the winter time, the local fishing boats switch their focus from catching slip soles to scallops, so we follow their lead. You can use a griddle plate or an overhead grill (broiler).

Serves 4

· 4 large live scallops, in their shells
· 60 g/2 ¼ oz Seaweed Butter
 [pp. 226]
· pinch of sea salt

Preheat a griddle pan or overhead grill (broiler). Remove the scallops from their shells and thoroughly clean the lower shell.

Divide the seaweed butter among the lower shells and sit the scallop back on top. (If you are using an overhead grill then put the butter on top of the scallop).

Cook the scallops in the shells on a griddle (or under the grill) for around 4 minutes, until the butter has melted. Turn the scallops over in the shell and baste them. Cook for a further 1 minute, or until the scallops are almost done to medium-rare. Turn them and baste them again, so they are well coated with buttery juices. Season lightly and serve straight away in the shells.

Raw scallops

In the restaurant we tend to use smaller scallops for this dish,
allowing one per person.

Serves 4

· 4 scallops, roes separated
· walnut oil
· Apple Balsamic Vinegar [pp. 242]
· Seaweed Powder [pp. 246]
· Scallop Roe Powder [pp. 246]
· few celery leaves, finely shredded
· sea salt

Slice the scallops crosswise into thin rounds – you should get 5 slices from each. Arrange them on a plate, rather like the Olympic rings, and add 2 drops of walnut oil to each slice of scallop. Add a drop of apple vinegar to each slice and season each with a little seaweed powder. Use a judicious hand here: a good pinch will do each plate. Now sprinkle each with a little scallop roe powder and top with a few shreds of celery leaf. Finish with a pinch of salt and serve straight away.

Slip sole

There was a gap between the discovery of seaweed butter [pp. 226] and putting it on the menu – it took a while to work out what to do with this butter. It didn't seem right on the bread board. Then one day, we were cooking slip soles in the kitchen. I took a slice of the butter, put it on the sole and grilled it for about four minutes. I rested it for about the same amount of time, basting twice. Slip sole is a great local fish and we used to serve them simply grilled with tartare sauce at the oyster company – because they are cooked on the bone, they have a gelatinous texture and need resting time. The result was perfect, but I still asked myself if it needed acidity or any kind of garnish – the answer to both was no. In fact, if anything was added it would distract from the main event and the dish would not taste as good. Just as if you go into a gallery and there is one piece on a white wall you will concentrate on it – minimalism.

I took some time to meditate on the aromas. A friend from the wine trade had said he couldn't believe there was no truffle in the dish and I found I could also detect truffle, along with vanilla. These are two of the most expensive ingredients used in a commercial kitchen, but here I had this ingredient growing right outside the pub – and it was free. Over the years it's become one of our best-loved dishes.

Slip sole
in seaweed butter

I liked the idea of serving the fish alone on a plate. It was a statement of intent. And it was provocative – I knew I would get people saying it needs some vegetables or potatoes. But I disagreed, people just needed to concentrate on the fish, reunited with seaweed on a plate with the help of a bit of butter.

Serves 4

· oil, for greasing
· 4 x 250 g/9 oz slip soles, skinned and heads removed
· 8 x 15 g/½ oz discs Seaweed Butter [pp. 226]
· sea salt

When ready to cook, preheat an overhead grill (broiler) and arrange the slip soles on an oiled and lightly seasoned griddle pan. Cut thin slices of the seaweed butter and arrange a couple of slices on each fish. Place under the grill for 3–4 minutes. Baste at least once to ensure each fish is completely covered with the butter. You should see some signs of shrinkage at the bones.

Remove the fish from the grill (broiler) and leave to finish cooking on the hot pan for a further 3–4 minutes.

Season very lightly and serve straight away.

Pickled herrings

This recipe may seem like it makes a lot, but the herrings will keep in the pickling solution in the refrigerator for up to two weeks.

Makes 12

· 12 herring fillets (make sure they are bright and shining)
· around 55 g/2 oz (½ cup) sea salt
· around 55 g/2 oz (½ cup) caster (superfine) sugar

Pickling solution
· 180 ml/6 fl oz (¾ cup) Apple Balamic Vinegar [pp. 242]
· 80 g/3 oz (¾ cup) caster (superfine) sugar
· 4 juniper berries
· 4 peppercorns
· 1 bay leaf
· 1 small carrot, thinly sliced
· 1 small red onion, thinly sliced

Place the herring fillets in a shallow tray and sprinkle over a light layer of salt and sugar. Cover with clingfilm (plastic wrap) and leave in the refrigerator for 12 hours. Rinse them well and pat dry.

Combine the vinegar and sugar with 120 ml/4 fl oz (½ cup) filtered water in a measuring jug and stir until the sugar has dissolved.

Put the herrings in a non-metallic container (plastic or porcelain is good) and add the juniper, peppercorns, bay leaf, carrot and onion. Pour on the liquid and cover with clingfilm (plastic wrap). Leave the herrings to pickle in the refrigerator for a week before eating, then store in the refrigerator for up to two weeks.

Herring on soda bread

We serve these as snacks on the tasting menu, varying the jelly according to the season. We serve gooseberry in the summer, rhubarb in the spring and crab apple in autumn.

Serves 6 as part of a tasting menu

· 1 slice Soda Bread [pp. 232]
· 1 tablespoon cream cheese
· Apple Jelly [pp. 242]
· 1 large Pickled Herring fillet
  [pp. 106]

Spread the soda bread thickly with cream cheese and spoon on a layer of apple jelly.

Cut the bread slices and the herring fillet into 6 x 2 cm/¾ inch squares. Sit a piece of herring on top of each square of bread and fix with a cocktail stick.

Pickled herring and cabbage salad

This simple, sharp salad works beautifully
with the lightly spiced herring.

Serves 4

· 400 ml / 14 fl oz (scant 2 cups)
  Apple Balsamic Vinegar [pp. 242]
· ½ white cabbage, finely shredded
· ½ red cabbage, finely shredded
· 1 red pepper (capsicum), diced
· 1 small bunch parsley, chopped
· 1 clove garlic, crushed
· 4 Pickled Herring fillets, sliced,
  plus vegetables from the pickling
  liquid, to serve [pp. 106]

Mustard dressing
· 1 heaped tablespoon Dijon
  mustard
· 1 tablespoon Apple Balsamic
  Vinegar [pp. 242]
· 300 ml / 10 fl oz (1 ¼ cups)
  neutral oil
· sea salt

Soda breadcrumbs
· 2-3 slices Soda Bread [pp. 232]
· 1 tablespoon butter

Heat the vinegar until boiling. Put the grated white cabbage and red cabbage into separate mixing bowls and pour in the hot vinegar. Add the pepper (capsicum) and parsley to the white cabbage, then divide the garlic between the red and white cabbage and mix each salad together well.

To make the dressing, mix the mustard with the vinegar and gradually whisk in the oil, as if you were making a mayonnaise. Season to taste.

To make the soda breadcrumbs, blitz the bread in a food processor to fine crumbs. Melt the butter in a frying pan, then add the breadcrumbs and fry until crisp.

Put a decent-sized blob of mustard dressing on each serving plate, followed by a spoonful of each cabbage salad, vegetables from the pickling liquid and a spoonful of breadcrumbs. Top each portion with the herring fillet slices and serve.

Thornback ray

Back in 1998, while working in a local fish restaurant, I was interested to see the different types of skate that were brought in by the fishermen. One type – blonde skate – had a very pale skin and a slightly woolly texture. Occasionally they'd bring us a different type, which had darker skin and a firmer texture. This variety also had thorns on its back, no doubt to offer protection from predators. The thorns (I later learnt they are known as 'bucklers') were calcified and once removed resembled miniature curling stones, with the tip of the thorn mimicking the handle.

I also discovered that the thornback was a much superior fish. Rather than the texture being open and woolly when cooked, the flesh of the thornback was denser and stickier on the teeth. As a result, I would always ask the fishermen for thornback ray rather than blonde skate. It suited the fish to be roasted rather than poached and I was then able to offer something different from the ubiquitous brown butter and caper sauce every other restaurant served.

I wanted to keep the brown butter because it made such a delicious base to a sauce, but I thought I could get the acidity from a very good quality sherry vinegar. And indeed there was something special about the nuttiness of the butter paired with the oaky acidity of the vinegar. I felt that cockles would also enjoy being with vinegar, in the same way they are served on fish stalls outside pubs in London. I added parsley to cut the richness of the sauce and bring a green freshness to the dish.

As an interesting footnote, many years later I was working with an archaeologist and he was baffled as to what these little calcified 'buttons' were that they found in abundance at the site of Canterbury's fish market. I was able to solve the mystery and tell him that they were the 'bucklers' from thornback ray. It was reassuring to have evidence that this was a fish that had been eaten in the area for at least a thousand years.

Thornback ray
with cockles and brown butter

If you can't find thornback ray, this will
still work with skate or another ray.

Serves 4

· 4 x 200–250 g/7–9 oz portions
  thornback ray
· sea salt
· groundnut (peanut) oil,
  for frying
· 125 g/4 ½ oz (½ cup) butter
· 300 g/11 oz cockles, cooked,
  shelled and grit removed
· 1 tablespoon sherry vinegar
· small bunch flat-leaf parsley,
  finely chopped
· squeeze of lemon juice
· Sautéed Cabbage [pp. 240],
  to serve

Preheat the oven to 120°C/235°F. Season the ray all over with salt. Pan-fry each fish in a little oil, thicker side down, until golden brown.

Transfer to a baking pan and cook in the oven for about 15 minutes. Check the fish is just done by carefully inserting a knife into the flesh near the cartilage. It should be barely cooked. Season the fish again and leave to rest while you make the sauce.

Heat the butter in a smallish pan until it is nut brown and smells 'toasty'. Now you need to act quickly. Take the pan off the heat, add the cockles and shake them around. Add the vinegar and parsley, shake again, then check the seasoning. You will need to add a pinch of salt and a squeeze of lemon juice.

Serve the fish, thicker side up, on some sautéed cabbage and spoon over some of the sauce.

Turbot

Floating around in the back of my mind I have always had the idea of constructing an entire meal from one whole fish, such as turbot, although I know it would be difficult to achieve this in the day-to-day running of a restaurant kitchen. For example I would serve a broth made from the bones, seaweed and beach herbs, as we do with our Rockpool dish [pp. 94], then I would serve the cheeks braised in seaweed butter, the skin could be made into a cracker, the skirt of the fish could be served deep-fried with tartare sauce and, finally, the fillet could be served with a sauce made from the fish roe.

When I was visiting New York in 2010 I had a great meal at Per Se restaurant and among the dishes was a sensational red mullet served with its own roe. Red mullet is an unusual fish in that its liver has always been regarded as a delicacy, but I hadn't realised that the roe was so good. I was particularly excited by this dish because in the UK it always seems that cod's roe is the only one used – maybe because they are very large and easy to smoke.

Anyway, when I arrived back home to Kent it was early spring and several of the turbot that were delivered to the restaurant kitchen had roe in them. Many chefs are disappointed when they open up a fish and find roe because you are paying for something you wouldn't normally use. And there are also some chefs who think the quality of the fish is not quite as good when they are carrying roe, although I can't say I have ever noticed this. Not daunted – and inspired by my meal at Per Se – I decided to smoke some of the turbot roe overnight and see if I could use it in a sauce.

The next day I melted some of our home-smoked butter in a small pan, being careful not to overheat it. Then I split the smoked roe sacks open, scraped out the tiny eggs and added them to the pan, stirring gently until I had an emulsion. I left the whole thing to set in the refrigerator and then, to serve, I melted the smoke roe into some warm velouté and served it with the turbot fillets. The result was so good that it has been a regular on the menu ever since. The fish and its roe back together on the plate.

Turbot
with a smoked roe sauce

Serves 4

· 4 x 125 g/4 ½ oz turbot or brill
  fillets
· salted butter, for greasing
· Apple Balsamic Vinegar [pp. 242]
· 1 tablespoon crème fraîche

· Smoked roe sauce
· Smoked salt butter [pp.227]
· roe of the turbot or brill, salted
  for 30 minutes, then rinsed

Pickled celeriac
· ½ celeriac, peeled and julienned
· generous pinch of salt
· 1 tablespoon Apple Balsamic
  Vinegar [pp. 242]

Start preparing the sauce at least a day ahead of time. Put the crème fraîche for the butter and the roe into a smoker (separately) and leave overnight, or for a minimum of 10 hours. After smoking the crème fraiche, chill until cold. At the same time, put the bowl of a stand mixer into the refrigerator to chill. Reserve 1 tablespoon of the crème fraîche.

The next day, make the smoked salt butter.

Weigh the smoked roe sacks then, with a very sharp knife, carefully split them from top to bottom, using the back of the knife to gently scrape out the eggs. They tend to hold together in one big waxy lump, but you will easily see the thousands of tiny individual eggs.

Weigh the roe, then weigh out twice the amount in smoked butter and place in a small pan. Melt it over a gentle heat, making sure it doesn't split. Add the roe and beat with a spoon to form an emulsion. Cover and leave to set in the refrigerator.

Place the celeriac in a bowl with a couple of pinches of salt. Leave for 15 minutes and then mix through the vinegar and a splash of water. Drain just before you serve.

When you are ready to serve, preheat an overhead grill (broiler) and butter a non-stick pan. Arrange the fish in the pan and dot with a few knobs of butter. Grill for about 3 minutes. Add a splash of the apple vinegar to the pan and stir it into the cooking juices. Baste the fish then remove it from the grill (broiler) and leave to finish cooking in the residual heat while you finish the sauce.

Warm up the tablespoon of reserved crème fraîche in a small pan then add the chilled smoked roe butter. Stir gently, taking care not to overheat it. Just before serving add another splash of apple vinegar, to taste.

Baste the fish with its pan juices a final time, then top with some pickled celeriac. Pour on the smoked roe sauce and serve straight away.

Brill braised in vin jaune with smoked pork

This is a very popular dish at The Sportsman, which works well with brill or turbot. This recipe actually began life as turbot braised in vin jaune with morels, but because fresh morels are so hard to get we changed to using smoked pork. That being said, we do prepare the dish with mushrooms, when in season.

Serves 4

Smoked pork
· 200 g/ 7 oz Confit Pork Belly
  [pp. 154]

Braised brill
· 25 g/1 oz (1 tablespoon)
  soft butter
· 4 x 125 g/4 ½ oz brill fillets
· 175 ml/6 fl oz (¾ cup)
  vin jaune
· 200 ml/7 fl oz (scant 1 cup)
  Fish Velouté [pp. 239]
· 50 g/2 oz (¼ cup) cold butter
· lime juice
· salt
· steamed broccoli florets, to serve

For the smoked pork, place the confit pork belly in a cold smoker and smoke overnight. Reserve until required.

When ready to cook the fish, preheat a griddle and an overhead grill (broiler). Divide the pork belly into 4 portions and cook on the preheated griddle until golden brown all over.

Meanwhile, lightly butter a non-stick frying pan and heat on the stove top. Add the fish and pour on 125 ml/4 fl oz (½ cup) of the vin jaune. Dot the surface of each fillet with a little soft butter and season with a good pinch of salt. Cook under the grill for about 4 minutes, basting with the wine a few times. When the fish is almost cooked, remove the pan from beneath the grill and keep the fish covered and warm. It will finish cooking in the pan.

Transfer the juices to a small pan. Add the rest of the vin jaune and bring to a boil. Boil rapidly to reduce by half. Add the fish velouté to the pan and bring back to a boil. Simmer until reduced to a coating consistency. Add the cold butter to the pan and blitz with an immersion blender. Add a good squeeze of lime juice and a pinch of salt to taste.

To serve, arrange the fish fillets in shallow bowls and pour on the sauce. Place the steamed broccoli next to the fish, place the smoked pork slices on top of the fish and serve straight away.

Meringue ice cream, sea buckthorn, sea water and seaweed powder

It is very difficult to come up with desserts for the tasting menu, especially in the winter. In summer we have such good fruit that there is never a problem, but between Christmas and the first fruit of the new year the cupboard is pretty bare. This dessert bridges the gap as it uses sea buckthorn berries and seaweed from the beach – and even seawater. Most importantly, it tastes delicious. We have to tell customers to eat all of the elements together as the buckthorn is so mouth-puckeringly acidic that it only works when combined with the other ingredients.

Serves 4

Meringue ice cream
· 500 ml/17 fl oz (generous 2 cups) double (heavy) cream
· 700 ml/24 fl oz (scant 3 cups) full-fat (whole) milk
· 400 ml/14 fl oz (1 ⅔ cups) Sugar Syrup [pp. 241]
· 1 teaspoon rosewater
· Meringue [pp. 214], roughly crumbled

Seawater spray
· 200 ml/7 fl oz (scant 1 cup) seawater
· ½ teaspoon caster (superfine) sugar

· 80 ml/2 ½ fl oz (⅓ cup) sea buckthorn juice*, to serve
· Crystallised Seaweed Powder [pp. 245], to serve

For the meringue ice cream, combine all the ingredients, except for the meringue, in a blender and blitz at high speed. Transfer to the refrigerator and chill for at least an hour. Pour into an ice cream machine and churn according to the manufacturer's directions. Transfer to a plastic container and freeze for at least 2 hours before serving. When the mixture is still a bit soft, fold in the crumbled meringue and return to the freezer.

For the seawater spray, dissolve the sugar in the seawater and put into a spray dispenser.

To serve, drizzle a little sea buckthorn juice in the bottom of serving bowls. Top with a quenelle of meringue ice cream and spritz with a little seawater. Add a good sprinkle of crystallised seaweed powder and serve straight away.

*sea buckthorn juice is available from online suppliers.

The Salt Marshes

The Thames Estuary and Seasalter Marshes

The Thames Estuary and Seasalter Marshes

The river Thames begins in Gloucestershire and winds its way through Oxford, Windsor and London before flowing past Seasalter, and the land surrounding The Sportsman, out into the North Sea. Its estuary runs from Greenwich in the south east of the capital to Margate on the Kent coast and is a good environment for shellfish; the beds just off the beach in Whitstable are home to some of the best native oysters in the world, available between September and April. There are other shellfish found here such as rock oysters, which are available year round, cockles, whelks and winkles, which are of course put to use in our kitchen, but the bay has undoubtedly become synonymous with native oysters over the centuries. In 1793, an act of parliament created a co-operative oyster company, which was to be responsible for the town's wealth and fierce independence. The company was owned by its workers and the profits would be divvied up on the 26th July – the feast of St. James, the patron saint of shellfish. There is an oyster festival every year on this day, but unfortunately native oysters are out of season in the summer. Many a visitor has questioned why there would be an oyster festival when the product is out of season – I have to agree.

The estuary coastline is nearly all made up of marshland and provides perfect grazing for sheep. Outside the pub, this flat landscape is punctuated by mounds of earth, which were a continuous mystery for my friends and I as our train from school rattled across the marsh from Whitstable to Faversham. As eleven year olds in the first year of secondary school studying Dark Age history, we concluded that the mounds must be Anglo-Saxon burial grounds like the one in Sutton Hoo, East Anglia. When it came to our second year, however, the content of our Geography lessons captured our imaginations, and these mounds became drumlins (hills of compacted clay) formed by the last Ice Age. That was before we realised that the ice never quite made it as far south as Seasalter.

The mystery remained for many years until a customer sent me a report on an archaeological dig of the area that a friend of his had carried out in the 1950s. Historically, it was an important area for making salt, and the dig report revealed that the mounds were old saltworks, covered by earth over time. Further evidence showed that a road through the woods to Canterbury from Seasalter was known as the 'salt road'. Of course, the marshland would have been very important in the days when access to large amounts of salt meant the ability to preserve food and live through the winter.

Salt

One of the questions I am always asked is why we make our own salt. My stock answer is that any chef who lives in a place called Seasalter and doesn't try making his own salt is asleep on the job. If I came from Bakewell, I am sure I would have made Bakewell tarts.

The Sportsman's (and my) adventure with salt began back in 2000, when someone went into our local deli, Williams & Brown, and asked if they would like to buy Seasalter salt. The deli owner, David Brown, asked me if I would be interested in such a product, and I said yes I would, but we never heard any more about it.

By 2004 I was beginning to develop the idea of serving a tasting menu made solely of ingredients that surrounded the pub. I remembered the story of the man who was going to revive the local salt industry and I asked around to see if anyone knew who or where he was, but he had disappeared. I believed that the idea was too good not to pursue. I loved the idea of eating a meal cooked with salt from the sea outside our very own pub. There seemed to be only one thing for it, and that was to go down to the sea, collect some water and make it myself.

I had seen an advertisement from the nineteenth century for 'marine boiled salt' from Whitstable, so I figured that would be the appropriate method to use. I also looked at the image on the side of a box of Maldon salt, depicting a person raking salt crystals. These were my guides as I walked along the estuary to where it meets the sea with a bucket.

I filled it with salt water, returned to the kitchen and boiled the water until it was almost all gone. Next, I poured the super-saturated salt water into a flat container… and then the magic happened: a white crust of salt began to crystallise on the surface of the water. I gently skimmed the surface and removed perfectly white, delicate salt crystals – every bit as good as any fleur de sel I had seen.

I put the concentrated water back onto a low heat and more crystals appeared. By the end of this process I had collected a decent amount of white salt crystals and some sludgy grey salt as well. In that moment I knew that I would be able to make enough salt to season everything on the tasting menu.

Salt-baked gurnard with braised fennel

I have always liked the idea of gurnard more than the reality. It is nearly always roasted and served with crisp skin, but I find the skin to be bitter. One day I thought I would try to bake it in a salt crust, and the results were extraordinary: the flesh was sweet and saline, and had a pleasing gelatinous texture.

Serves 4

· 2 medium gurnard (about 1 kg/ 2 lb 4 oz) each), gutted and cleaned
· 1 kg/2 lb 4 oz (5 cups) sea salt (I use sel gris)

Braised fennel
· 1 large fennel bulb, outer leaves removed
· 1 tablespoon olive oil
· shot of Pernod
· 150 ml/5 fl oz (⅔ cup) fresh orange juice
· squeeze of lemon juice
· sea salt

Preheat the oven to 200°C/400°F. Spread a thin layer of salt over the bottom of a heavy baking pan. Arrange the fish in the pan with space between them. Cover entirely with the rest of the salt, although it's not necessary to cover the heads or tail tips. Sprinkle with a little water to dampen the salt completely.

Bake the fish for 15 minutes per kg/2 lb 4 oz, plus an additional 2 minutes. Use a probe thermometer to check that the thickest part of the fish has reached 45°C/115°F. Now remove from the oven and leave the fish to finish cooking in the residual heat for at least 10 minutes – although they will happily keep out of the oven in the salt for up to 30 minutes.

While the fish are baking, prepare the fennel. Slice the bulb in half lengthwise and cut out the core. Slice thinly widthwise and reserve the fronds separately. Heat the oil in a large frying pan. Sauté the fennel over medium heat for around 10 minutes, or until it starts to brown. Deglaze the pan with the Pernod and cook until it evaporates. Add the orange juice to the pan (holding back 1 tablespoon) and cook until it evaporates and the fennel is sticky. Remove from the heat and add the reserved orange juice, a squeeze of lemon juice and a good pinch of salt.

After the fish have rested, the salt will have cooled to form a hard crust, which can be easily cracked away and removed. Use a pastry brush to brush away any residual salt from the fish, then transfer them to a board and carefully peel away the skin. Use a sharp knife to remove the 4 fillets; keep them in one piece if you possibly can. Remove any pin bones with tweezers.

Serve the fillets on the braised fennel, and garnish with the reserved fennel fronds.

Oysters

The town of Whitstable was pretty much built on oysters. In 1793, Parliament awarded the Whitstable Oyster Company a charter to exploit the shoreline and a co-op was formed. The 'free-dredgers' were the workers of the oyster company and this progressive system meant that the profits were shared between them. On the feast of St.James – July 26th – the workers would hold an annual meeting above the Duke of Cumberland. At this meeting, the profits were doled out and the town would become the scene of a pretty debauched party.

When disease and overfishing damaged the oyster beds in the mid-20th century, the company fell into disuse until it was revived by the Green family in the 1980s. We are so lucky to be right next to some of the finest oyster beds in the world that it would be crazy not to celebrate them. As a result I decided to serve an oyster course on the tasting menu.

There is a certain type of food bore who makes proclamations about whether you should cook oysters or not. These people are just trying to make themselves appear knowledgeable and seem to want to impose their narrow view of the world on every-body. With this in mind, we decided to serve both raw and cooked oysters.

When The Sportsman first opened I wanted to serve oysters, but in an original way. Every place in town served them the same way with shallot vinegar, Tabasco and lemon. I had some chorizo in the kitchen and remembering oysters basquaise – a dish of cold oysters with spicy sausage – I just put a disc of grilled chorizo on a cold oyster and we had an interesting and original way of serving them.

Then one Christmas, myself, my partner Emma and a big group of friends decided to celebrate together. I wanted to serve some snacks at the beginning of the meal, and remembered the great oyster dish by Marco Pierre White with cucumber and caviar, so tried to copy it. I was astonished at how long one mouthful of food can take for all the different tastes to resolve themselves in your mouth.

I decided to do my own version, which also referenced 'oysters and pearls' from Thomas Keller's The French Laundry.

Oysters and chorizo

We use native oysters to make this dish, and it's as simple as it sounds.

Makes 10

· 10 slices chorizo, around
  5 mm/¼ inch thick
· 10 native oysters, chilled and
  freshly shucked

In a dry frying pan, sauté the chorizo slices on each side until lightly browned and, while they are still hot, put on top of the cold oysters and serve straight away.

Poached rock oysters with apple granita and seaweed

This recipe changes with the seasons. In summer we will use gooseberry granita and in the spring we use rhubarb. In winter we use apple.

Makes 10

· 10 rock oysters
· Seaweed Powder [pp. 246]
  (a pinch on each oyster)
· 50 ml/2 fl oz (¼ cup) double
  (heavy) cream (a teaspoon for
  each oyster)
· edible rose petals, finely shredded
  (when in season)

Apple granita
· 2 Bramley apples, unpeeled,
  quartered and cored
· ½ teaspoon ascorbic acid

To make the apple granita, use a centrifugal juicer to juice the apples. Dissolve the ascorbic acid in a tablespoon of the juice, then stir it back into rest of the juice. Pour into a small, shallow container and freeze. Stir every few hours and, once frozen solid, scrape with a fork to create a granita consistency.

When ready to serve, shuck the oysters (reserving the shells) and put them into a frying pan, along with their juices. Heat gently and just before the liquid boils, remove from the heat and leave for 2 minutes.

To assemble the dish, arrange the oyster shells on a tray lined with cockle shells. Return the warm oysters to their shells and top each one with a teaspoon of cream. Add a pinch of seaweed powder and a teaspoon of granita. Finish with a few strands of rose petal (if using) and serve straight away.

Poached rock oysters with pickled cucumber, beurre blanc and avruga caviar

This is not real caviar but a smoked herring product made to look like caviar.

Makes 10

Beurre blanc
· 1 shallot, chopped
· 100 ml/3 ½ oz (scant ½ cup) white wine
· 100 ml/3 ½ oz (scant ½ cup) Apple Balsamic vinegar [pp. 242]
· 300ml/10 fl oz (1 ¼ cups) double (heavy) cream
· 250 g/ 9 oz (scant 1 cup) butter, chilled and cubed
· lime juice
· sea salt

Pickled cucumber
· 1 small cucumber
· 200 ml / 6 fl oz (1 scant cup) Apple Balsamic vinegar [pp. 242]

· 10 rock oysters
· 2 tablespoons avruga caviar

Make the beurre blanc by putting the chopped shallot into a small saucepan over a medium heat with the wine and vinegar. Reduce until it has almost all gone. Add the cream, bring to the boil, and simmer for 5 minutes.

Strain the cream into a jug and add the chilled butter. Blitz with a hand blender until smooth. Adjust the seasoning with lime and salt; it needs to be very sharp as it is fighting for attention with the others components.

Now pickle the cucumber – this should be done at least 1 hour in advance. Using a mandolin, cut the cucumber into thin strips like linguine. Place in a small bowl, add a pinch of salt and leave for 10 minutes.

Rinse the cucumber strips and add the vinegar. Leave for 20 minutes then strain the cucumber.

Shuck the oysters, reserving the shells. In a small frying pan over a low heat, warm the oysters with their juice. Just before the juice boils, take the oysters off the heat.

To assemble, put the warm oysters in their shells and spoon over a tablespoon of beurre blanc. Place a tangle of cucumber on top and then a small scoop of the avruga caviar.

Angels on horseback

I don't know the true origins of this dish, but I have heard some Whitstable locals claim it for the town. As children we used the same name to describe sardines on toast.

Makes 4

· 4 native oysters
· 4 thin slices dry-cured streaky (lean) bacon
· groundnut (peanut) oil, for deep-frying
· Parsley Purée [pp. 244], to serve

Shuck the oysters and place them in a small bowl. Pour on enough boiling water to cover them and leave for 1 minute. Transfer to a bowl of cold water. This has the effect of firming the oysters ready for the next stage.

Lay the slices of bacon on a board and use the back of a knife to scrape them to make them thinner still. Arrange an oyster at one end of each bacon slice, then roll up and secure with 2 cocktail sticks.

Heat the oil in a deep fryer to its highest temperature. Fry the oysters for 1 minute. It can be helpful to make one extra and test the timing: they should be crisp on the outside and creamy in the centre.

Allow to cool briefly on paper towels, which also helps them crisp up. Remove one of the cocktail sticks and serve with parsley purée.

Lamb's kidney on brioche

When you buy whole animals, as we do, it is necessary to find ways of using every part. I am also a great believer in following the old habit of eating the offal (variety meats) immediately. I think many people have convinced themselves that the uric tang of kidneys is desirable, but it actually means you are eating old offal. We cook kidneys within two days of slaughter and they taste creamy and fresh. They come covered with fat, which protects the meat during cooking.

Makes 6–8

· 1 small Brioche [pp. 234]
· 1 teaspoon goose fat
· 1 lamb's kidney, with fat
· Homemade Butter [pp. 224]
· Apple Sauce [pp. 242], to serve

Preheat the oven to 180°C/350°F. Cut the brioche into 6 slices and toast on both sides. Allow to cool, then trim into 2 cm/¾ inch squares.

Melt the goose fat in a small ovenproof tin. Sauté the kidney over medium heat until golden brown, then transfer to the oven for 10 minutes. Remove from the oven and leave the kidney to finish cooking in the residual heat for 10 more minutes.

Cut the butter into thin slices, to fit the brioche squares then place on top.

Carve the kidney into slices and arrange on the brioche squares. Top with a blob of apple sauce and serve straight away.

Braised lamb shoulder

Although we call this braised lamb shoulder, it's actually confit with a sauce made separately and brought together at the end. It regularly features as the main course on the tasting menu.

Serves 6

· 2 kg/4 lb 4 oz lamb shoulder
· 2 sprigs of rosemary
· 6 cloves garlic, bruised
· a good handful of sel gris
· 1.5-2 litres/34 fl oz (6 ¼ cups) duck fat

Roast lamb gravy
· 1 tablespoon neutral oil
· 500 g/1 lb 2 oz lamb trimmings
· 1 large onion, roughly chopped
· 1 head of garlic, split in half crosswise
· 1 large carrot, roughly chopped
· 100 g/3 ½ oz button mushrooms, finely sliced
· 100 g/3 ½ oz cherry tomatoes, blitzed to a liquid
· 100 ml/3 ½ fl oz (scant ½ cup) white wine
· 1 litre/34 fl oz (4 ¼ cups) chicken stock [pp. 239]
· 1 small onion, grated
· 1 small carrot, grated
· 1 celery stalk, grated
· 1 large sprig rosemary
· 1 star anise
· 1 clove garlic, crushed
· piece of cold butter
· squeeze of lemon juice

· Mashed Potatoes or Potato Gratin [pp. 238], to serve
· Green Beans [pp. 240], to serve

Remove the front leg of the lamb at the shoulder joint, or ask the butcher to do this for you.

Put the lamb into a half-sized gastronorm pan, deep enough to hold the shoulder, and sprinkle over the rosemary and garlic. Scatter the salt evenly over the lamb shoulder, cover and leave in the fridge for 36 hours.

Remove from the fridge and wash off the salt, garlic and rosemary from the lamb, and clean the container.

Preheat the oven to 100°C/210°F. Warm the duck fat and pour a layer into the gastronorm container. Place the washed shoulder back into the container and pour over the rest of the fat to cover. Loosely cover with wax paper. Cook the lamb in the oven for 10-12 hours.

Allow the shoulder to cool in the fat. When still soft you must remove the shoulder blade without disturbing the shape too much. Wrap the shoulder in clingfilm (plastic wrap) to maintain the shape and put in the fridge over-night to set.

When ready to serve prepare the gravy. Heat the oil in a large pan and sauté the lamb trimmings until golden brown.

Add the onion, garlic, carrot and mushrooms to the pan and stir well. Deglaze with the cherry tomato juice. Cook until the tomato liquid has dried and is starting to caramelize.

Deglaze with the wine and continue cooking until it has evaporated.

Deglaze again with the chicken stock, then bring to a boil. Lower the heat and simmer for 1 hour. Strain and return to a clean pan. Boil rapidly until the liquid is reduced by three-quarters. Taste and season if need be.

Add the grated vegetables, the rosemary, star anise and garlic and leave to infuse for 15 minutes. Strain. Reheat before serving and whisk in the cold butter and a squeeze of lemon juice at the last moment.

In a frying pan, reheat the lamb in a little duck fat, cooking until crisp. Cut into slices and serve with the gravy, potatoes of your choice and green beans.

Lamb breast and mint sauce

This is a small snack, which we serve as part of the tasting menu just before the lamb main course. I am always conscious that English food is considered quite bland, so I like to present this as a way of showing how exciting it can be. The crisp breadcrumbs, the heat of the mustard and the cooling effect of the mint put you in mind of Southeast Asia rather than England. By turning the lamb breast into finger food and serving it with a mint dipping sauce, it also demonstrates the importance of presentation.

Serves 6–8 as part of a tasting menu

· 1 whole lamb breast
· sel gris
· 4 sprigs fresh rosemary
· 6 garlic cloves, roughly crushed

Crumb coating
· groundnut (peanut) oil, for
  deep frying
· 200 g/7 oz (1 ¾ cups) plain
  (all-purpose) flour
· 3 eggs, beaten
· 200 g/7 oz (scant 3 cups) slightly
  dried breadcrumbs
· Dijon mustard, to coat

Mint sauce
· 200 g/7 oz (1 cup) demerara
  (turbinado) sugar
· 200 ml/7 fl oz (scant 1 cup) malt
  vinegar
· 1 small bunch mint, finely
  chopped

Use a very sharp knife to remove the rib bones from the breast in one swooping motion. Cut the breast into two even portions.

Scatter a layer of sel gris over the bottom of a deep roasting tin, just large enough to contain the meat comfortably. Arrange the lamb pieces in the pan, and cover evenly with more salt. Cover with cold water and refrigerate for around 6 hours so the meat can brine.

Drain off the water then rinse the lamb pieces and pat dry with paper towel. Vacuum-pack the breast pieces (in 2 bags) with the garlic and rosemary and cook, sous-vide, at 82.2°C/180°F for around 12 hours.

Remove from the water bath and let the meat cool, flat, as quickly as you can. Remove from the vacuum bag and separate the pure meat from the sinews. Cut the meat into strips, a bit like 'soldiers'.

For the mint sauce, Bring 200 ml/7 fl oz (scant 1 cup) water to a boil in a small pan. Stir in the sugar, to dissolve, then boil for 5 minutes. Leave to cool completely before adding the vinegar and mint.

When ready to serve, preheat a deep fryer to 180°C/350°F. Arrange shallow bowls of flour, beaten egg and breadcrumbs on your work counter.

Coat the lamb strips generously in mustard, then coat them in flour, egg and breadcrumbs. For a really crisp result it is important to achieve even single layers of each coating, rather than crumbing them twice.

Deep-fry the lamb in batches for around 3 minutes, or until crisp and golden brown. Transfer to a wire rack and allow to cool slightly. Pat dry with paper towel. Serve with the mint sauce.

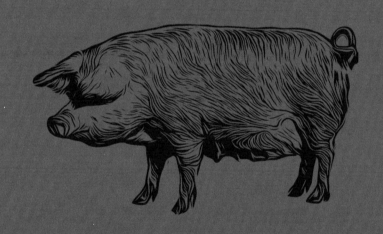

The Farms

Elham Valley, Monkshill
and Beyond

Elham Valley, Monkshill and Beyond

Although I grew up in Whitstable, before opening The Sportsman I wasn't aware of how much agriculture existed around me; driving around the area, the first thing I noticed was how many farms there were.

As the salt marsh turns into hills, which lead to the Blean – the local name for the woods – there were several farms that defined the landscape. The lines of cabbages, fruit trees, geese running in formation between August and December – these sights reminded me of the south west of France, which got me thinking about 'cuisine de *terroir*'.

I was fascinated by Pierre Koffman's book *Memories of Gascony*, and had loved the gutsy but restrained food served at La Tante Claire. It wasn't poncey and was rooted in something real – it reflected the countryside, even though it was served in Chelsea.

The use of goose fat, chickens, plums and cabbages seemed to suit the landscape that surrounded me, and I was determined to let the locally produced ingredients guide my menus. If I added the produce of local farms onto the seafood that the area is famous for, then I had a good start in creating a 'cuisine de *terroir*' for the area around my pub.

I am always suspicious when chefs take over a place in the country and say immediately that they get all of their ingredients from the local producers. It wasn't that easy for me. It takes time – often years – to develop a strong relationship with a farmer.

For this relationship to be mutually beneficial, I believe a restaurant kitchen has to be committed to a certain way of working. From the beginning, I realised that we had to have a standing order with the farmers for them to be guaranteed an income. It was no use just demanding some lamb and then changing the menu because I felt like cooking something else that week. I had to align my whole menu to the farm's produce.

So, every week, Mr Mckeever from Waterham farm would deliver a dozen chickens, which we would break down into legs and breasts, then make stock with the bones. This became the routine on which the kitchen's whole week was formed. And every week, Monkshill farm would deliver three lambs. I have to emphasise that at the time, most restaurants didn't work like this. At the other places I had observed, the chef would phone the butcher after service and order, for example, 20 lamb rumps. The butcher's job was to try to guess what the restaurant would use.

Building our kitchen around the local ingredients felt like the right thing to do. Over the last 16 years, the knock-on effect has been that problems can be quickly resolved, we have an input into the way our ingredients are grown, and it's given the kitchen a routine, creating a kind of order within the chaos.

Sadly Mr Mckeever, the chicken and geese farmer, died along with his great knowledge, and the next generation only carried on briefly before selling up.

Also, recently Monkshill farm went bust, despite its thousand-year history. Small-scale farming is a labour of love, which often means long hours for a poor return. However much we try to make things work for the farmer, life tends to get in the way.

Now we are working closely with Ottinge farm, in the nearby Elham Valley. It is a dairy farm that still produces unpasteurised milk and cream, but because they are caring farmers who work on a small scale, the lambs and pigs are also fantastic. As I write, this cycle that has formed the basis of how we cook at The Sportsman has begun again; we are building this relationship and allowing their ingredients to dictate our menu.

Bacon

We started to buy whole pigs from Monkshill farm in around 2003 and it meant that we suddenly had a new problem to solve. How were we going to use the whole animal? The breeds varied from middle whites to Oxford sandy blacks but the quality was astonishing. The meat was tender and firm but still had that farmyard flavour. We could even influence how much fat the animal developed.

In the autumn we took batches of windfall apples and pears and fed them to the pigs. The fruit could be tasted in the fat of the animal. It used to depress me when I would see the odd plate coming back from the restaurant with the fat left. Why did people think that the fat from a well looked after pig was bad for them? Did they believe that the fat from the animal would turn into fat on them?

We wouldn't be knocked off course and Phil, my brother, would tell customers that we liked to serve the fat – it was deliberate, a policy. This is another gripe I had about fine dining at the time. It was so sanitised that they would trim the life out of any ingredient. The meat would usually be a cylinder of fat-free protein from something like the fillet or tenderloin and pork was seen as not even worthy of a fine restaurant. To add to this they would cut things up into tiny bits so as to ensure that the flavour was lost. I started to think that we could not only compete with the best restaurants in London, but we could better them. If we used the same techniques as them but with far superior ingredients then surely our food would be much better.

The problem I now had was what to do with every bit of the animal. We used the obvious cuts such as the loins and belly but the legs were proving a problem. I would cook them on a Saturday lunch and serve them with pease pudding – it was delicious but it didn't sell. I think people thought it was too ordinary to order in a restaurant. History then provided the answer. I looked into the ways of curing that were used in the Middle Ages and I realised that they would slaughter the pigs in early November. This was the best time for many reasons – the animal had eaten well in the easy days of summer and would be dispatched before feed got scarce in the winter. Also, the meat would be cured, hence the value of salt on the marshes, and then hung to last through winter.

To follow this idea, I started to cure my own hams in the style of Jabugo ham from Spain. I had seen hams that had been boned out, which appealed to me as I didn't have the room to cure lots of hams on the bone. The results were fantastic – hams that had umami by the bucket load, that lovely shine as they were cut from the fat.

To use the other cuts, we also made our own bacon. I had always loved dry-cured bacon since I had eaten it from Marks & Spencer, and when I made this simple cure it was a revelation.

An idea was beginning to emerge. There were lots of products that are made on a large scale in factories which were poor compared to making things myself. The bacon and butter were two great examples, and so I set out to find other products that were better made in small batches, without the tricks or preservatives of industrial food production.

Maple-cured bacon

A large plastic tub or Tupperware container is useful for this recipe.
You want it to be just larger than the pork. Once cured, the bacon
will keep, refrigerated, for 2–3 weeks.

Makes 1.2 kg/2 lb 8 oz

· 1 x 1.5 kg/3 lb 5 oz boneless
  pork loin
· 500 ml/17 fl oz (generous 2 cups)
  maple syrup
· 600 g/1 lb 5 oz (3 cups) sea salt
  (I use sel gris)

Rub the pork all over with the maple syrup. Put into a plastic tub, cover with
a lid or clingfilm (plastic wrap) and refrigerate for 2 days. Turn several times.

Remove the pork from the plastic tub and wipe it out (but don't wipe the
pork itself). Return the pork to the tub, skin-side down, and cover with half
the salt. Cover again and refrigerate for 2 days.

Rub the salt off the pork, then return it to the tub, skin-side down, and cover
with the rest of the salt. Return to the refrigerator for another day.

Rinse the pork thoroughly and pat very dry. Hang in a cool place for 3 days.
The pork is now ready to use, as you would bacon. Store in the refrigerator
once cut.

Mussel and bacon chowder

This recipe came about because I wanted to find a way of using our homemade bacon without making a big deal of it. I loved the idea that customers would order the soup without thinking the bacon was anything special, and then they'd be taken by surprise – just as I was the first time I tasted it. The bacon's sweet maple cure, along with the dry-salting, makes quite an impression, even in such small amounts as are used here. I love the mussel stock in moules marinière and although we initially used this for the chowder I felt the warm alcohol flavour was not welcome. We changed to cooking the mussels just in plain water, and the soup was perfect. The scallop roe powder adds an intriguing acid-umami element.

Serves 4

· 1 kg/2 lb 4 oz mussels, scrubbed and 'beards' removed
· 4 slices Maple-Cured Bacon [pp. 150]
· 2 medium potatoes, peeled
· 100 g/3 ½ oz (½ cup) butter
· 4 leeks, finely chopped
· sea salt
· 250 ml/8 fl oz (1 cup) crème fraîche, plus extra to serve
· 2 tablespoons fresh breadcrumbs (we use leftover soda bread)
· 2 tablespoons finely chopped chives
· Scallop roe powder [pp. 246], to serve (optional)

Start by cooking the mussels. Measure 200 ml/7 fl oz (scant 1 cup) of water into a large pan and bring to a boil. Add the mussels, cover the pan and cook for around 3 minutes, or until all the shells have opened. (Discard any that refuse to open.) Leave the mussels in the pan to cool, then strain the stock into a bowl and set aside. Remove the mussel meat from the shells and set aside.

Pan-fry the bacon slices until golden, then remove from the heat, allow to cool and cut into batons. Reserve with the mussel meat.

Cook the potatoes in boiling water until soft, then drain.

To prepare the soup, combine the butter and leeks in a large pan and add a splash of water and a pinch of salt. Cook over a medium heat until the leeks are soft, but still bright green. If the water evaporates entirely, add another splash.

Break the potato up roughly and add it to the pan. Pour in enough of the reserved mussel stock to cover the vegetables by around 5 cm/2 inches. Top up with water, if necessary. Cook vigorously for 2 minutes.

Remove the pan from the heat and carefully pour into a blender. Blitz until smooth, then add the crème fraîche and blitz again. Taste and adjust the seasoning. You are aiming for the smooth thickness of a good winter soup, so if too thick, adjust with a little milk.

To serve, divide the reserved mussel meat and bacon among warmed soup bowls. Pour on the hot soup (which will heat them sufficiently) and finish with a sprinkling of chopped chives and breadcrumbs, a small dollop of crème fraîche and a scattering of scallop roe powder, if using.

Pork belly and apple sauce

This method is exactly the way we make it in the restaurant kitchen and you won't get the same results with the recipe scaled down. Sometimes we smoke the confit pork belly, to serve with Brill Braised in Vin Jaune [PP. 120], and we use the trimmings to make Pork Scratchings [PP. 156].

Serves 8–10
as part of a tasting menu

Confit pork belly
· 1 x 2 kg/4 lb 8 oz pork belly, bone in
· Good handful of sel gris
· 3 litres/100 fl oz (12 cups) duck fat
· Apple Sauce [pp. 242], to serve
· Mashed potatoes [pp. 238], to serve
· Sautéed Cabbage [pp. 240] or steamed spinach, to serve

Sit the pork belly in a large roasting pan and rub the salt into the pork flesh. Put the pan into the refrigerator and pour in enough water to cover the meat completely. After 12 hours, take out of the refrigerator and pour away the water. Rinse well.

Preheat the oven to 100°C/210°F. Put the duck fat into a large pan and melt it slowly. Pour a layer of fat into the roasting pan and arrange the pork belly on top, skin side down. Pour in the rest of the fat and cover loosely with greaseproof (wax) paper. Cook for 12 hours.

After 12 hours, check that the pork belly is cooked by pulling at a rib bone. If it doesn't move freely, then return to the oven for another 20 minutes and check again.

Remove from the oven and leave to cool. You can strain off the duck fat to be used again. Transfer the pork belly to the refrigerator and leave overnight to set hard.

Remove the bones and trim the edges to create a neat rectangle. Keep the trimmings to make the pork scratchings.

Cut the belly in half down the middle and then divide into portions as you wish. We get 8–10 main course portions from one belly. Wrap the individual portions in clingfilm (plastic wrap) until they are needed.

When ready to serve, preheat the oven to 180°C/350°F and take the belly portions out of the refrigerator.

Arrange the belly portions in a non-stick, ovenproof frying pan and loosely cover with a baking paper. Roast for 20 minutes, then remove from the oven. If the skin isn't nicely browned, then finish on direct heat on the stove. Remember the skin is like glass: it will be gel like when hot, but will crisp up as it cools. Turn the portions over and leave to cool slightly before serving with apple sauce, mashed potatoes and cabbage.

Pork scratchings

Pork scratchings are, of course, a standard snack in many English pubs, but my inspiration for this recipe came from a meal at Noma restaurant in Copenhagen. Back in the winter of 2006–2007 I remember being served chicken skin as a snack at the beginning of their tasting menu. This was a landmark idea at the time and my mind turned to the pork scratchings that I used to make for fun at The Sportsman – although the idea of serving them as anything other than a bar snack had never crossed my mind. But eating René Redzepi's crisp chicken skin made me think, why not offer a version of the humble pork scratching at the start of our own tasting menu? It would be perfect for an English pub restaurant. We serve our scratchings with a dipping sauce made from equal quantities apple sauce and wholegrain mustard.

Serves 4–8

· Pork belly trimmings [pp. 154]
· Groundnut (peanut) oil, for deep frying
· Apple Sauce [pp. 242]
· Wholegrain mustard

The pork belly trimmings will be two long strips of mainly fat; cut these crosswise into 5 mm (¼ inch) slices, leaving on the skin.

Set a deep fat fryer to its highest setting. When it reaches temperature, add the pork slices in batches, cooking for 1–2 minutes, or until they are golden brown. Be careful, because the fat can spit as water is released.

Drain the scratchings on paper towels and allow to cool slightly before serving with their dipping sauce.

Whole roast pork loin

Cooking meat on the bone and in larger pieces produces results that can't be matched. The meat contracts and expands but loses no juice. Ask your butcher to remove the chine bone but to leave the ribs attached, and make sure the skin is soft to touch. If it is too dry you won't be able to make good crackling.

Serves 4–6

· 1 x 1.5 kg/3 lb 5 oz pork loin, trimmed (reserve the trimmings for the gravy)
· sea salt
· 1 tablespoon goose fat
· Apple Sauce [pp. 242], to serve
· Mashed potatoes [pp. 238], to serve
· Sautéed Cabbage [pp.240], to serve

Gravy
· 1 tablespoon groundnut (peanut) oil
· 500 g/1 lb 2 oz pork trimmings
· 1 onion, finely chopped
· 1 carrot, finely chopped
· 2 celery stalks, finely chopped
· 1 star anise
· 175 ml/6 fl oz (⅔ cup) white wine
· 150 g/5 ½ oz cherry tomatoes, blitzed to a liquid
· 1 litre/34 fl oz (4 ¼ cups) chicken stock [pp. 239]
· piece of cold butter
· squeeze of lemon juice

To prepare the pork loin, score the skin with a very sharp knife and rub in a tablespoon of the sea salt.

Put the goose fat into a large, ovenproof, non-stick frying pan and heat gently to melt. Put the pork into the pan, skin side down, and cook over low–medium heat for 20–30 minutes, or until the skin is crisp and golden. I weigh the meat with another heavy pan so all the skin is in contact with the heat.

Meanwhile, preheat the oven to its highest temperature.

Season the pork all over with salt and roast for 5 minutes. Lower the temperature to 130°C/250°F. Roast for around 50 minutes then check the internal temperature with a probe thermometer. When it reaches 50–55°C/120–130°F remove from the oven and rest in a warm place; it will increase by 5–7°C/40–45°F with the residual heat. Rests for 30 minutes.

While the pork is roasting and resting, prepare the gravy. Heat the oil in a large pan and sauté the trimmings until golden brown. Add the vegetables and star anise to the pan and stir to help lift up all the bits of caramelised pork. Cook over a medium heat until all the vegetables are nicely browned.

Deglaze with the wine and continue cooking until it has evaporated. Deglaze with the cherry tomato juice. Cook until the tomato liquid has dried and is starting to caramelise.

Deglaze again with the chicken stock, then bring to a boil. Lower the heat and simmer for 1 hour. Strain and return to a clean pan. Simmer until reduced to around 200 ml/7 fl oz (scant 1 cup). Taste and season if need be.

To serve, you will need to remove the rib bones. This should be fairly straight-forward as the meat will have cooled as it rests and a sharp knife should slip under the ribs easily. Allow the bones to guide the knife and slice them away. If the meat beneath is a little pink, then give it a flash under a hot grill (broiler). Season lightly and carve into slices with the crackling attached.

Warm the gravy and whisk in a piece of cold butter and a little lemon juice. Taste and adjust the seasoning, then serve with the pork and accompaniments.

Warm chocolate mousse, milk sorbet and salted caramel

I had always wanted to serve a warm mousse, and I found further inspiration for the idea back in 2005, when I was flicking through the elBulli cookbook one day. In my version, I began by spooning salted caramel into a coupe glass, then topped it, elBulli-style, with foaming warm chocolate from an iSi whipper. Because I always like to serve contrasting tastes, the dark chocolate demanded a milky flavoured ice cream. I put a scoop on top and it slowly sank into the warm mousse as it arrived at the table. This was perfect: both delicious and theatrical.

Serves 6–8

Caramel
· 175 ml/fl oz (¾ cup) double (heavy) cream
· 125 g/4 ½ oz (⅔ cup) caster (superfine) sugar
· sea salt

Milk sorbet
· 500 ml/17 fl oz (generous 2 cups) double (heavy) cream
· 700 ml/24 fl oz (scant 3 cups) full-fat (whole) milk
· 400 ml/14 fl oz (1 ⅔ cups) Sugar Syrup [pp. 241]
· 1 teaspoon rosewater

Chocolate mousse
· 225 ml/8 fl oz (1 cup) double (heavy) cream
· 380 g/13 ½ oz 70% chocolate, roughly chopped
· 225 g/8 oz (1 cup) egg whites

Start by making the caramel. Heat the cream to just below boiling, then remove from the heat. In another pan, heat the sugar until it melts and turns dark brown. Take off the heat and pour in the hot cream. Be careful as it may spit. Return to the heat and warm gently to ensure the caramel is completely dissolved. Allow to cool then cover and refrigerate for up to a week.

For the milk sorbet, combine all the ingredients in a blender and blitz at high speed. Transfer to the refrigerator and chill for at least 30 minutes. Pour into an ice cream machine and churn according to the manufacturer's directions. Transfer to a plastic container and freeze for at least 2 hours before serving.

To make the chocolate mousse, heat the cream in a pan until it starts to simmer. Add the chocolate to the hot cream, take off the heat and whisk gently to amalgamate. Add the egg whites to the chocolate cream mixture and whisk by hand again to incorporate.

Pour into an iSi whipper and fit with two N20 cream chargers. Sit in a 65°C/150°F water bath for 1 hour before using, shaking every now and then to equalise the temperature.

We serve this dessert in glass ice cream coupes. Start by putting a tablespoon of caramel in the bottom of each coupe and add a pinch of salt. Shake the iSi whipper, lower the nozzle to just above the caramel and squirt in the chocolate mousse, keeping the nozzle beneath the mousse as it emerges. Fill to 2 cm/¾ inch below the top of the coupe. Leave for 1 minute, then carefully sit a scoop of sorbet on top. It will stay in place for a few minutes before slowly slipping in, so serve it straight away.

The Woodlands and Hedgerows

The Kent Weald

The Kent Weald

The landscape of Kent changes from flat marshland to forest, pastures and rolling hills as you leave the north coast and head south past Canterbury. The is area known as the Weald of Kent, and is the upland between the North and South Downs National Park stretching through to Sussex and Hampshire. The forest traditionally provided pannage for pigs, and the green fields were home to cattle, often the native Sussex breed.

I remember going to Simon Hopkinson's Bibendum restaurant in the early nineties and having raw Jersey cream with my fruit tart for pudding. I asked the waiter about the cream and he said it came from the cheese and dairy suppliers, Neal's Yard. The next day, I made my way to their shop in Covent Garden and sure enough they had small green and white tubs of raw Jersey cream from a farm in Kent.

I can't begin to tell you how good this cream was. It was dense, thick and yellow, and tasted of farmyards, iron and roses – I knew then that a great restaurant should be based around this kind of ingredient. It had the same name as ordinary cream, but just eating a small spoonful would send me into a trance as I tried to analyse what I was tasting, and it changed as I contemplated it; one second sweet, the next mineral, the next floral.

When I got a head chef job at a pub in the Weald I decided to try to find the farm. The side of the tub had said White House Farm, Biddenden, so I took it upon myself to drive to the village.

I met a lady called Rosemary Sergeant who showed me around. The sight that remains with me from that day was the herd of beautiful, healthy Jersey cows chomping away on the dark, green, damp grass, before they were happily led to the milking sheds. It left a deep impression on me because I started to think that being a chef was almost pointless. How could I make anything as beautiful as this product? How could I beat some strawberries just picked from a local field, served with the unpasteurised cream from these magnificent beasts? From that moment on, I resolved to create dishes that would allow this exceptional produce to shine, and what's more, to never allow my ego or technique get in the way.

This got me thinking. It encompassed more than the lush pastures, the marshes and the bounty from the sea. The area around the pub has always been good for game (which is why it is called The Sportsman), and we have found evidence from the early twentieth century of shooting parties blasting teals, partridges and even a golden merganser from the sky. In Autumn, the hedgerows on the nearby roads are filled with tart but sweet blackberries, and come May, the elderflower trees around the pub blossom, which we use in elderflower posset with elderflower fritters.

The tricks and clumsiness of chefs just seemed to pale next to these ingredients. I pondered the idea that this could be the base of our cooking at The Sportsman. Just as the great olive oil of Provence and the pastures of Normandy dictate the flavours of regional French cooking, so we too could make a style that was the taste of Kent.

Mushroom and celeriac tart

I wanted to serve a tart at the beginning of our tasting menu that looked the same as the chocolate tart that we served at the end, but tasting completely different. It doesn't look anything like the chocolate tart, but it's a great recipe.

Makes 6

Mushroom mix
· 10 g/¼ oz dried ceps
· 50 g/2 oz (¼ cup) butter
· 250 g/9 oz chestnut mushrooms, finely diced
· sea salt
· few drops of truffle oil or grated black truffle
· 20 g/¾ oz grated Parmesan
· squeeze of lemon juice
· a little double (heavy) cream, if required
· 6 egg yolks

Celeriac purée
· 50 g/2 oz (¼ cup) butter
· 300 g/11 oz celeriac, peeled and diced
· sea salt
· 100 ml/3 ½ fl oz (scant ½ cup) full-fat (whole) milk

Cabbage crisps
· 1 Savoy cabbage, outer leaves discarded
· vegetable oil, for deep-frying

Pastry cases (shells)
· 200 g/7 oz (1 ⅔ cups) soft pastry flour
· 100 g/3 ½ oz (½ cup) cold butter, diced
· pinch of sea salt
· 2 tablespoons double (heavy) cream

Celeriac foam
· 380 g/13 ½ oz Celeriac Purée (above), chilled
· 225 ml /8 fl oz (1 cup) double (heavy) cream, chilled
· 225 g/8 oz (1 cup) egg whites, chilled

Cep Powder [pp. 247], to serve

For the mushroom mix, first soak the ceps in hot water (enough to cover) for around 15 minutes. Strain the liquid and reserve. Chop the ceps finely.

Heat the butter in a pan until nut brown and it smells 'toasty'. Add the mushrooms. Sauté for 10 minutes, then add the soaking liquid. Add a pinch of salt and a little truffle oil and sweat on a medium heat until the moisture has evaporated. Remove from the heat and allow to cool. Stir in the Parmesan then check the seasoning and adjust with salt and lemon juice, to taste.

For the celeriac purée, melt the butter in a pan, then add the celeriac and a pinch of salt. Sweat on a medium heat until soft but not completely cooked. In a separate pan, heat the milk to a gentle simmer, then pour over the celeriac and simmer for 2 minutes. Tip into a blender and blitz to a smooth purée. Pass through a sieve and allow to cool. Refrigerate until required.

To make the crisps, blanch the cabbage leaves then pat dry and leave to cool. Turn the oven on to its lowest temperature. Arrange the leaves on a baking sheet and leave overnight until they have dehydrated and become crisp.

For the pastry cases (shells), mix the flour and butter together until they resemble breadcrumbs. Add the salt and cream and knead until you have a pliable dough. Wrap in clingfilm (plastic wrap) and refrigerate for at least 30 minutes. Preheat the oven to 180°C/350°F. Remove the pastry from the refrigerator and roll out to 5 mm/¼ inch thick. Line 6 x 8 cm/3 ¼ inch non-stick tart cases with the pastry and bake for 25 minutes, until golden.

About 1 hour before serving, make the celeriac foam. Whisk the cold ingredients together with the celeriac purée until smooth. Pour into an iSi whipper and fit with two N20 cream chargers. Sit in a 65°C/150°F water bath for 1 hour, shaking every now and then to equalise the temperature.

Preheat the oven to 80°C/175°F. Warm the mushroom mixture, loosening with a little cream if needed. Divide among the cases. Make a dent and carefully add the yolks. Bake for 10 minutes, then remove from the oven. While the tarts are baking, deep-fry the dehydrated cabbage leaves until crisp. Drain well on paper towels then crumble into rough pieces.

To serve, lift the tarts onto plates, then cover evenly with celeriac foam. Dust the surface of each tart with cep powder and finish with cabbage crisps.

Partridge and celeriac 'risotto'

Partridge has a delicate flavour, which is creamy with a hint of almonds, and when I first combined it with celeriac it was immediately clear that it is a great pairing. It is rare that two plus two equals five – but this is one of those rare occasions.

Serves 4

· 2 x oven-ready partridges
· piece of butter
· sea salt and pepper, to season

Celeriac 'risotto'
· 1 medium celeriac (about 700 g/ 1 lb 9 oz), scrubbed
· 2 celery stalks, chopped
· 150 g/5 ½ oz (⅔ cup) unsalted butter
· 1 tablespoon grated Parmesan
· squeeze of lemon juice
· 1 tablespoon finely chopped chives
· 1 tablespoon finely chopped celery leaves
· sea salt and pepper, to season

For the 'risotto', first peel the celeriac, making sure you keep all of the trimmings. The next stage is to cut the celeriac into rice-sized 'grains'. To do this, first cut it in half, for ease of handling. Cut each half into thin slices, then cut the slices lengthwise into long narrow strips, then crosswise into 'grains'. Reserve any trimmings.

Next, make a stock. Roughly chop the reserved celeriac peel and trimmings into small pieces. Put in a pan with the chopped celery and add enough filtered water to just cover. Bring to a boil, then lower the heat and simmer for 20 minutes. Strain, then return the stock to the pan and simmer until reduced by half. Set aside until needed.

When ready to cook the partridges, preheat the oven to 120°C/235°F.

Melt the butter in a baking pan and brown the birds all over. Season with salt and pepper, then roast for 15 minutes. Remove from the oven and leave to rest for 10 minutes.

While the birds are resting, make the celeriac 'risotto'. Keep the stock at a simmer. In another pan, melt 50 g/2 oz (¼ cup) of the butter. Add the celeriac 'rice' and sauté over medium heat for a few minutes, until slightly softened, but not coloured. Add the stock, a ladleful at a time, until the celeriac is cooked (around 5 minutes). It should be tender, but still have some bite.

While the celeriac is cooking, preheat an overhead grill (broiler) to its highest temperature and carve the partridges. Slice away the breasts and arrange them on a baking sheet. Just before serving, crisp the skin of breasts under the grill and season lightly. Pick the meat from the carcass and keep warm.

Remove the pan of celeriac from the heat and beat in the rest of the butter. Stir in the cheese and the reserved partridge scraps, then add a squeeze of lemon juice and the chopped herbs. Taste, and adjust the seasoning.

Divide the risotto among 4 warm bowls and serve with the crisp-skinned partridge breasts on top.

Baked cod with chestnuts, parsley and bacon

One year I was looking for a fish dish to put on our Christmas menu. I have loved chestnuts since I was a small boy, when I used to walk past the old men selling them from their charcoal braziers, and the smell always puts me in a festive mood. Their sweetness meant that I needed a salty element – and I never need too much of an excuse to get out my own bacon. When I added the fresh flavour of parsley the whole thing seemed to come together.

Serves 4

· 4 x 200 g/7 oz cod fillets
· 2 thick-cut slices Maple Cured Bacon [pp.150]
· 50 g/2 oz (4 tablespoons) Homemade Butter [pp. 224], plus extra for greasing
· 12 chestnuts, peeled
· 100 ml/3 ½ fl oz (scant ½ cup) chicken stock
· sea salt
· squeeze of lemon juice
· Parsley Purée [pp. 244], to serve

Salt the cod fillets all over and leave in a colander in the sink for 20 minutes. Rinse and pat dry.

Meanwhile, pan-fry the bacon until crisp and brown, then drain briefly on paper towels, cut into batons and keep warm.

Add a tablespoon of the butter to the same frying pan and gently sauté the chestnuts for around 10 minutes until they are tender and evenly browned. Add the chicken stock and simmer until the stock has evaporated to create a lovely glaze. Remove from the heat and keep warm.

Preheat an overhead grill (broiler) to high and lightly butter a medium non-stick frying pan.

Arrange the fish in the buttered pan and top each with a piece of butter, reserving a tablespoon for making a sauce. Grill (broil) the fish for around 3 minutes, basting often with the browning butter. Once the fish is nearly cooked, remove from the grill (broiler) and leave in a warm place to finishing cooking in the residual heat. Reserve the juices, adding a squeeze of lemon juice to create a sauce.

To serve, make an artful swoosh of parsley purée on each plate. Dress the fish fillets with the buttery lemon sauce, adding another squeeze of lemon juice and a little seasoning to each. Place the fish on top of the parsley purée, then top with the reserved bacon and chestnuts. Drizzle on any remaining sauce and serve immediately.

Note: To peel the chestnuts, use a sharp knife to make a cross in the skin and deep-fry them for 2 minutes. They should then peel easily. Alternatively roast in a medium oven for 15 minutes, or simmer in boiling water for 15 minutes.

Pheasant, bread sauce, rose hip juice

I remember dining at Michel Bras' restaurant in the Aubrac and listening to the waiter explain about a sauce that was made with bread, as if it were revolutionary. It was unusual in France but in the UK, we often eat bread sauce alongside roast poultry and game.

Serves 4

· 2 pheasants, on the crown
· sea salt
· 2 tablespoons goose fat

Bread sauce
· 500 ml/17 fl oz (generous 2 cups) full-fat (whole) milk
· 1 medium onion, roughly chopped
· 6 cloves
· 1 bay leaf
· couple of twists of pepper
· 100 g/3 ½ oz (⅔ cup) slightly dried breadcrumbs
· freshly grated nutmeg, to taste
· sea salt and black pepper
· 80 g/3 oz (⅓ cup) butter

Rose hip juice
· 300 ml/10 ½ fl oz (1 ¼ cups) Sugar Syrup [pp. 241]
· 500 g/1 lb 2 oz rose hips, picked after the first frost

Deep-fried cabbage
· 1 Savoy cabbage, or cavolo nero, shredded
· vegetable oil, for deep-frying

To make the bread sauce, put the milk into a small pan and add the onion, cloves and bay leaf. Leave to infuse overnight.

Strain and heat to simmering point. Add the breadcrumbs and stir until the sauce thickens. Season with nutmeg, salt and pepper to taste. Just before serving, whisk in the butter. Don't just drop it in and leave it to melt. You need to whisk it in so it emulsifies, rather like making a risotto.

For the rose hip juice, bring the sugar syrup to a boil in a medium pan, then add the rose hips. Simmer for 30 minutes, then remove from the heat and leave for 3 hours to infuse.

Strain the syrup and bring it back to a boil. Boil rapidly until it thickens. To test the consistency, spoon a few drops onto a cold plate and refrigerate for a minute. If it holds firm on the plate – a bit like making jam – it is ready.

Heat a deep fryer to 180°C/350°F. Fry the shredded cabbage or cavolo nero in batches until crisp. Drain on paper towels and season.

To cook the pheasant, first preheat the oven to 100°C/200°F and season the meat with salt.

Heat the goose fat in a heavy roasting pan and brown the pheasant all over. Roast for 30 minutes, or until a probe thermometer reads 60°C/140°F. Remove from the oven and rest for at least 15 minutes.

Remove the breasts from the breast bone and slice each one in thirds.

Put a spoonful of hot bread sauce in the centre of each warmed plate and arrange the pheasant on top. Drizzle the rose hip juice around and serve with the deep-fried cabbage or cavolo nero.

Raw venison, pickled turnip and crisp cavolo nero

This dish takes a lot of customers by surprise because it looks fairly ordinary until you actually eat it. It was born out of the need to get the most out of very expensive venison and so we use the fillet from the inside of the saddle. This is the most tender meat on the whole animal. The uncooked venison is well seasoned, as it must be, and spread out over the plate like a carpaccio. The pickled turnip adds a dash of acidity, aided by the apple vinegar, and the crisp cabbage contrasts well with the softness of the uncooked meat. It produces a strange effect in the mouth as you experience both soft and crunchy simultaneously. In the summer we serve this dish with tomato, cheese and rocket, but I slightly prefer this winter version.

Serves 4

· 1 x 300 g/10 ½ oz venison fillet
· 1 small turnip, washed
· sea salt
· 1 teaspoon caster (superfine) sugar
· 2 tablespoons Apple Balsamic vinegar [pp.242], plus extra to drizzle
· pepper
· 1 cavolo nero, shredded into thin strips
· vegetable oil, for deep-frying

Sear the venison fillet over a high heat to brown it all over. It is a good idea to have a bowl of iced water to hand so you can dunk the pan in to stop the cooking.

Use a mandolin to shred the turnip into thin slices. Season with a few pinches of salt and leave for 15 minutes. Rinse and pat dry. Transfer to a small bowl.

Dissolve the sugar in the cider vinegar and 1 tablespoon water. Taste to ensure the sweet-sour balance is good, and pour over the turnip slices. Leave to infuse for at least 1 hour.

Slice the venison fillet into 12–16 thin slices. Place between sheets of grease-proof paper and use a rolling pin to bash them out even more thinly.

Divide the slices of venison among 4 plates (there should be 3–4 slices per portion). Scatter on the pickled turnip slices. Season generously and drizzle with a little apple vinegar.

Heat a deep fryer to 180°C/350°F. Fry the shredded cavolo nero in batches until crisp. Drain on paper towels and season. Scatter over the venison and serve straight away.

Elderflower posset and fritter

We have several large elderflower trees around us at the pub and I can't wait for the flowers to arrive in late-May, early-June. They signal the arrival of early summer and their optimistic smell fills the air – especially after a rain shower. Rather like asparagus, we like to binge on them while they are here, serving them in ice cream, cordial, possets and fritters. The fritter is the closest you will come to eating a doughnut without having to eat all that dough. When I see this dessert on its way out to a customer, I smile at the thought that the tree the elderflowers came from is only yards away – and the flower was still on that tree minutes before. This is us using ingredients in a way that most restaurants cannot match.

Serves 6

Elderflower possets
· 600 ml/21 fl oz (2 ½ cups) double (heavy) cream
· 70 g/2 ½ oz (⅓ cup) caster (superfine) sugar
· zest and juice of 1 lemon (or another citrus fruit)
· 1 head fresh elderflowers
· whipped cream, to serve

Elderflower fritters
· 100 g/3 ½ oz (¾ cup) self-raising flour
· 1 heaped teaspoon cornflour (cornstarch)
· 175 ml/6 fl oz (⅔ cup) soda water, chilled
· 1 tablespoon vodka
· good pinch of sea salt
· groundnut (peanut) oil, for deep frying
· 6 heads fresh elderflowers
· caster (superfine) sugar, to serve

For the possets, put the cream into a pan and bring to a boil. Take the pan off the heat and stir in the sugar until completely dissolved. Stir in the lemon juice and zest and the elderflower and boil rapidly for 90 seconds.

Remove from the heat and leave to infuse for 15 minutes. Strain through a sieve. Divide the cream between glasses and leave to cool fully at room temperature. Some people now refrigerate the possets until ready to serve, but I think the texture is more beguiling if they are allowed to set at room temperature for 2 hours. If it is a hot day you can give them 5 minutes in the refrigerator to begin to set, but no more than that.

To make the fritters, combine the flours in a mixing bowl and whisk in the chilled soda water. The batter should be the consistency of single (light) cream. If it is any thicker, the batter will be claggy. Gently whisk in the vodka and salt.

To deep-fry the fritters, first heat the oil in a deep fryer set to 180°C/350°F. Hold an elderflower by its stalk and dip into the batter, allowing most of it to drip back into the bowl. Lower gently into the oil. Repeat with the remaining elderflowers. Turn them around in the oil after 1 minute, then continue frying until golden brown. Remove from the oil and drain on paper towels.

While the elderflowers are frying, put caster (superfine) sugar into a shallow bowl. Toss the drained, warm fritters gently in the sugar, one at a time, and serve immediately alongside the possets, topped with a little whipped cream.

Wild blackberry lollies with cake milk

I find the idea of wild blackberries picked from the hedgerows and made into an ice lolly very romantic. Perhaps it's because most ice lollies are made in big factories. These are the link between the savoury and sweet part of the tasting menu – I suppose in the past they would have been described as a palate cleanser. We use a test tube set, which Sarah, our pastry chef found, to freeze the lollies.

Serves 6

· 150 ml / 5 ¼ fl oz (¾ cup) Sugar Syrup [pp. 241]
· 500 g / 18 oz (3 ½ cups) wild blackberries
· 1 teaspoon acsorbic acid
· test tube set

Cake milk
· 1 thick slice Madeira (pound) cake
· 400ml / 14 fl oz (1 ⅔ cups) full-fat (whole) milk
· 300 ml / 10 ½ fl oz (1 ¼ cups) double (heavy) cream

Heat the sugar syrup in a small pan until it is about to simmer, then add the blackberries off the heat and mush with the back of a fork. Leave to macerate in the fridge overnight.

The next day, strain through a sieve, then fill the test tubes with the blackberry liquid and freeze. When the mix is just set, put a wooden cocktail stick in each tube.

To make the cake milk, put the broken up cake and milk into a blender and blitz until smooth. Pour the mix into a bowl and add the cream, stirring until you have a thick liquid.

To serve, half fill 6 tall espresso cups or glasses with the cake milk. Unmould each lolly by dipping the test tube in hot water very briefly to release it. Put the lolly in each cup with the cake milk and serve immediately.

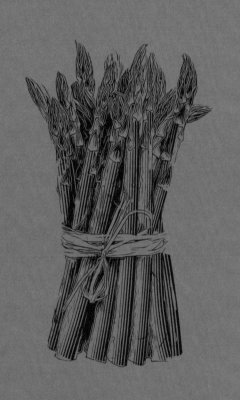

The Gardens

The Sportsman Allotment
and Isle of Thanet

The Sportsman Allotment and Isle of Thanet

We have several acres of land around the Sportsman that up until two years ago was a caravan site. We are now building wooden huts for people to stay in and we have set aside a large part of the land for growing our own produce.

We have been growing our own vegetables on a small scale for twelve years now, which would once have been enough for the tasting menu. Since then, though, the interest and number of people having the tasting menu has grown massively, and so we had to expand the operation. We have two large polytunnels and in the space between we have rows of beds where we can experiment with growing anything we like, from peas in summer to kohlrabi in winter.

It is logical to concentrate on produce that benefits from being extremely fresh, is more specialist or difficult to grow on a larger scale, rather than producing vegetables such as potatoes or cauliflowers that the farms grow very well just up the road on the Isle of Thanet. To pick small courgettes or peas and serve them within minutes is every good chef's dream. I love picking green beans and squeezing the sap between my fingers, just to show how fresh they are. The sap is slightly spicy and peppery. Once you've tasted freshly picked, you'll notice when it's missing – mostly evaporating due to age or cooked off due to bad technique – to me, that's when green beans are ruined.

Rather like buying direct from farms, growing vegetables has its own challenges. Courgettes, sorrel, broad beans, runner beans, rosemary and others grow very well in the soil at the pub, but some things just struggle. For example, we will never have a glut of peas, no matter how many plants we have.

When I was growing up on the fringes of Whitstable, there was a massive pea field at the end of our road and I can remember eating them straight from the pod when they were still quite small and warm. They were so sweet and tender that with that first taste I was spoilt for life – I still want to be able to pick them when they are very young rather than letting them get big, mealy and starchy. This seems to be a very English problem, as those from France and Italy are picked when they are still very small, hence petit pois. I have often bought peas in England and had to throw them away because they are inedible.

At the moment, I am working on using vegetables that are at the centre of a dish. Rather like you would have a piece of lamb or turbot, why not have a vegetable as the star. This is an idea that is growing around the world of restaurants, and we would like to develop more recipes with great vegetables at their heart.

I am pleased that this part of our menu is still a bit up in the air, because it means we are moving forward and not just repeating ourselves. A journalist who spent the day here once said that we still run our business like a start-up, and although I had never thought of it before, he is right.

To stand still is to be run over, and to be bored with such a great location would be a crime.

Crab, carrot and hollandaise

This recipe started back in 2005, before it had become a cliché to serve dishes in little Kilner jars, and was my attempt at playing with the concept of potted crab. I liked the idea of changing the preserving butter that you serve on the top of potted dishes for a fresh, foaming hollandaise, so I put some white crab meat, a bit of brown meat and some sorrel into a jar and covered it all with hollandaise. The dish was actually my idea of a culinary joke, but pretty soon those little jars began popping up everywhere and I decided it was time to move on. The next stage in its evolution happened in the summertime, when I was picking young carrots from the kitchen garden and was looking at ways of highlighting their natural flavour. We also had coriander (cilantro), which had flowered and run to seed, as well as fennel with its early pollen. I knew coriander and carrot were a classic match, and the fennel just lifted everything. So I put the dressed carrot in the bottom of a glass, topped it with freshly cooked crab and poured on my style of hollandaise, which is very foamy and acidified with citrus rather than vinegar. The result was so good that it has become one of our best dishes.

Serves 4

· 500 g/1 lb 2 oz white crab meat
[pp. 245]
· pinch of Scallop Roe Powder
[pp. 246]

Hollandaise sauce
· 2 egg yolks
· 150 g/5 ½ oz (⅔ cup) melted
  butter, kept warm
· pinch of cayenne
· pinch of sea salt
· squeeze of lemon juice

Carrot salad
· 2 medium carrots, grated
· 1 teaspoon fennel seeds, crushed
· 1 teaspoon coriander seeds,
  crushed
· 1 tablespoon Apple Balsamic
  vinegar [pp.242]
· good pinch of sea salt
· drizzle of olive oil

To make the hollandaise sauce, pour 45 ml/1 ½ fl oz (3 tablespoons) boiling water over the egg yolks and whisk vigorously to a froth. Now secure the bowl on a work top (a damp tea towel works well for this) and slowly add the warm butter, as if you were making a mayonnaise. Whisk continuously until it is all incorporated. Avoid any sediment that has sunk to the bottom of the melted butter. Once it is all incorporated, season with cayenne, salt and lemon juice. Keep at room temperature.

Combine the carrot salad ingredients in a mixing bowl and toss together.

Serve this in small glasses, as you would a seafood cocktail. Divide the carrot evenly, top each portion with the crab meat and pour on a generous amount of hollandaise sauce.

Cream of vegetable soup

I like the idea of understatement and it is used well here as the recipe title slightly downplays the diners' expectations by making them think of canned soup, but then delivers the sweetest, tenderest vegetables in a delicate, yet flavourful broth. The vegetables you use will depend on what is at its best at the time. In this recipe I give quantities for the ones we use in June. Whatever the season, to achieve the desired result, the most important thing is to pick the vegetables that same morning.

Serves 4 as part of a tasting menu

Mushroom stock
· 2 large onions, finely chopped
· 2 large carrots, finely chopped
· ½ head celery, finely chopped
· 2 large leeks, finely chopped
· 200 g/7 oz chestnut mushrooms, sliced
· parsley stalks
· 1 star anise
· 30 g/1 oz dried ceps
· 15 lemon verbena leaves, chopped

The soup
· 15 g/½ oz (1 tablespoon) Homemade Butter [pp. 224]
· 2 tablespoons freshly podded peas
· 2 tablespoons shelled broad beans
· 2 tablespoons chopped fine green beans
· 2 tablespoons chopped spring onion (scallion)
· sea salt and pepper
· 2 Sungold tomatoes, halved
· 8 small lemon verbena leaves
· shredded rose petals
· 200 ml/7 fl oz (scant 1 cup) sour cream
· good squeeze of lime juice

For the mushroom stock, put all the ingredients, except for the lemon verbena leaves, into a large pan. Pour on enough filtered water to just cover. Bring to a boil, then lower the heat and simmer for 15 minutes. Leave to infuse for 30 minutes.

Return to the boil, then simmer until the stock has reduced to about 250 ml/8 fl oz (1 cup). Add the lemon verbena and leave to infuse for 15 minutes. The stock can be made ahead of time and keeps well in the refrigerator for up to 4 days.

To make the soup, warm the butter in a non-stick frying pan. Add a tablespoon of water. Shimmy the pan to create an emulsion, then add the peas, beans and spring onion (scallion) and gently warm them up. It is crucial to note that you don't want to actually cook the vegetables, but merely to warm them – as if they have just been picked on a summer's day.

Once the vegetables are warm, season them and divide them among four small bowls. Add the Sungold tomato, verbena leaves and shredded rose petals.

Heat 500 ml/17 fl oz (generous 2 cups) of the mushroom stock in a small pan. Add the cream, then bring to a boil. Add a good squeeze of lime and check the seasoning. Blitz with an immersion blender until good and frothy, and divide among the four bowls.

Chilled asparagus soup

I first cooked this soup while staying with a friend in San Francisco. It was just an off the cuff idea, which I then brought back with me to the restaurant, only to be greeted by, 'Cold soup?!' Some people can't tell that it is asparagus; not because it doesn't capture the flavour, but because it is so unusual. This recipe actually brings out flavours you didn't know were there. For instance, there is a nutty dimension to asparagus that survives in the finished soup, which can often be lost in more aggressive treatments. To serve, I wanted to accompany it with something fairly neutral to give some contrast to the complex flavour of the soup itself. Just as a particular colour in a painting changes depending on the colours you put next to it, so it is with flavours. So I frothed some milk as you would when making coffee, and spooned the warm froth on top of the soup. It worked. Not just because of the temperature contrast but also because the neutral creaminess of the milk helped the complex, grassy, nutty soup to shine. A quick word about the technique: cutting the asparagus very thinly means that it cooks very quickly. This in turn means that more of the natural 'raw' flavours of the asparagus are preserved.

Serves 6

· 1 kg/ 2 lb 4 oz asparagus trimmings (these are the bits between the tips and the woody root)
· 1 tablespoon neutral oil
· sea salt
· 740 ml–1 litre/ 26–34 fl oz (3-4 ¼ cups) full-fat (whole) milk (enough to cover the asparagus in the pan, plus 250 ml / 8 fl oz (1 cup) extra, to serve
· 1 tablespoon crème fraîche

Slice the asparagus trimmings very finely.

Heat a large pan and add the oil. Add the asparagus trimmings and cook them rapidly, but without allowing them to brown. Add a couple of pinches of salt. Within a few minutes the asparagus will start to soften and turn bright green.

Meanwhile, bring the milk to a boil in a different pan. Pour it onto the asparagus, using just enough to cover. Simmer for 2 minutes then check that the asparagus is soft enough to purée: it should give when you squeeze a piece between your fingers.

Tip the asparagus into a blender and blitz, adding the milk gradually to ensure the consistency isn't too thin. Once smooth, stir in the crème fraîche then pass the soup through a sieve. If it is too thick, adjust the thickness with some more milk.

Chill the soup as quickly as possible so that the soup spends minimal time between 60°C–10°C/ 140–50°F. This helps keep the colour bright.

When ready to serve, froth the extra milk using a coffee machine or a hand frother. Pour the chilled soup into glass tumblers and then top with just enough frothed milk to cover the surface.

Salmagundi

I've always been drawn to the idea of a salmagundi. I love the word itself – it's the seventeenth century name for an English mixed salad – and of course I'm very keen on dishes that are truly seasonal, as it means I can focus my efforts on selecting produce at its very best, ideally straight from my own garden, instead of having to source ingredients from a supplier, which might not be up to the same standard.

Back in the early days of The Sportsman, while I was still dreaming of the perfect salmagundi, I visited Michel Bras' restaurant in the Aubrac plateau of France. One of his most famous dishes is the gargouillou – a salad that contains up to twenty different vegetables, all prepared separately. The waiter explained that the name comes from a traditional peasant soup, which can contain many different ingredients, depending on the season. I knew immediately that this would be the blueprint and inspiration for my own Sportsman salmagundi.

Back in the restaurant kitchen I gathered together as many ingredients from the restaurant kitchen garden as I could find, all in their prime. It was early July, which meant I was spoilt for choice: there were baby peas, broad beans, French beans, courgettes (zucchini), tomatoes and many other things, as well. And then it was a question of playing around with bits and bobs from the different sections of the kitchen. I selected some vegetable purées, a handful of fresh herbs and flowers, crunchy soda breadcrumbs, a buttery sauce, and I started to have some fun!

I began by decorating the plate with some artful smears of purée and topped them with a cooked baby carrot and a few cubes of roasted summer squash. Next, I flavoured the buttery liaison with a pinch of curry powder and warmed through my freshly picked vegetables: my aim was to maintain their intrinsic 'snappiness' – they didn't need to be cooked, just barely warmed through – and I wanted their sweetness to be enhanced by the earthy flavour of the curry. I arranged a poached egg on the plate, spooned over the warm vegetables and finished the dish with some leaves and flowers and a scattering of breadcrumbs, to represent soil from the garden. The end result was a visual delight, as well as being utterly delicious.

The joy of a dish such as this is the way it can be adapted to what's best during each season. Summer's glut provides a bounty, of course, but in the winter it works just as brilliantly with root vegetables and a smoked egg yolk. I thought about writing a recipe for this, but in the end, realised that it would be impossible. The best version will come from using this as a rough guide to create your own version from what you have available.

Pot-roast red cabbage

This recipe arose from a comment made by René Redzepi. He wondered why we chefs don't cook whole vegetables in the same way that we cook a chicken or other cut of meat: roasting, basting and so on. He experimented with roasting a whole cauliflower and that got me thinking about the way we cook vegetables at The Sportsman. I wondered why not pot-roast other vegetables. This recipe was my first attempt, and it's become a favourite on the menu.

Serves 4

· 1 medium red cabbage, tough
  outer leaves removed
· 150 g/ 5 ½ oz (⅔ cup) butter
· sea salt
· Apple Balsamic Vinegar [pp. 242],
  to serve
· 4 tablespoons cream cheese
· 1 tablespoon grated red cabbage,
  to serve

Stewed apple
· 2 Cox apples, unpeeled, cored
  and diced
· 100 g/ 3 ½ oz (½ cup) butter
· sea salt

Mustard dressing
· 2 tablespoons Dijon mustard
· 2 tablespoons Apple Balsamic
  Vinegar [pp. 242]
· 4 tablespoons neutral oil
· sea salt

Cut the cabbage in half and put in a heavy, cast-iron pan (I use an oval cocotte) with the butter and a good pinch of salt. Cover the pan and cook over a very low heat for 90 minutes, turning every half hour. Cooking over a low heat will steam the cabbage in the pot; too high a heat will burn the outside. Check with a small knife to see if the core is soft, and when it is ready, remove from the oven and leave to cool with the lid on.

While the cabbage is roasting, put the apples in a small pan with half the butter and cook gently for around 8 minutes, until soft. Stir in the remaining butter and add a pinch of salt.

To make the dressing, mix the mustard with the vinegar and gradually whisk in the oil, as if you were making a mayonnaise. Season to taste.

To serve, make artful squiggles of apple vinegar and mustard dressing on each plate. Put a spoonful of stewed apple in the centre. Slice each piece of still-warm cabbage in half and arrange one on each plate. Season lightly and top with a spoonful of cream cheese and a sprinkle of grated cabbage.

Steamed bass with cockles and summer pistou

To steam the fish, we sit it on a plate in a colander set above a pan of simmering water and cover with a lid.

Serves 4 as part of a tasting menu

· 4 x 125 g/4 ½ oz fillets wild bass (increase the size to 200 g/7 oz portions for larger main course size)
· sea salt
· 500 g/1 lb 2 oz cockles in their shells, well washed
· 12 thick spears asparagus, trimmed, tips removed and stems sliced into thin roundels
· 2 tablespoons fresh peas
· 2 tablespoons shelled broad beans
· squeeze of lemon juice
· drizzle of light Ligurian or Provencal olive oil

Summer pistou
· handful of basil leaves
· 1 tablespoon grated Parmesan
· 1 tablespoon olive oil

Season the fish fillets with salt, wrap them tightly in clingfilm (plastic wrap) and refrigerate for 2 hours to set the shape. Take out of the refrigerator 15 minutes before cooking.

Put a pan onto a medium heat and throw in the cockles. Cover and cook for 3 minutes, or until the shells have opened. Shake the pan from time to time to help the process. Leave the cockles in the pan to cool, then strain the juice and reserve. Remove the cockle meat from the shells and reserve.

To make the pistou, combine the ingredients in a mortar and pound to a paste. Alternatively, use a mini food processor.

Sit the fish fillets on a plate (still in their wrapping) and set in a colander over a pan of simmering water. Cover and steam for around 5 minutes, then check the internal temperature with a probe thermometer. When it reaches 45°C/110°F remove from the heat and leave to rest in a warm place; it will increase to just under 50°C/120°F with the residual heat.

While the fish is resting, heat the reserved cockle juice in a small pan. Add the asparagus rondels, peas and broad beans and cook for 2–3 minutes, adding a tablespoon of water if needed.

Meanwhile, heat a little water in a small frying pan and simmer the asparagus tips for 2 minutes. Drain and add to the pan with the rest of the vegetables. Stir in the pistou, then add the cockles and warm briefly.

To serve, divide the vegetables and cockles among 4 warm serving bowls. Dress the fish fillets with a little lemon juice and olive oil. Place on top of the cockle pistou and season. Serve straight away.

Rhubarb sorbet with burnt cream and shortbread

What takes people by surprise is that the rhubarb isn't cooked, so it's like biting into a stick of rhubarb dipped in sugar.

Serves 6

· Rhubarb sorbet
· 2 kg/4 lb 8 oz rhubarb stalks
· 400 g/14 oz (2 cups) caster (superfine) sugar

Burnt cream
· 425 ml/15 fl oz (1 2/3 cups) double (heavy) cream
· 1 vanilla bean
· 6 egg yolks
· 60 g/2 ¼ oz (5 tablespoons) caster (superfine) sugar, plus extra for the topping

Shortbread
· 280 g/10 oz (2 1/3 cups) soft pastry flour
· 1 tablespoon rice flour
· 2 good pinches of salt
· 250 g/9 oz (1 cup) cold diced butter
· 110 g/3 ¾ oz (½ cup) caster (superfine) sugar

To serve
· space dust (popping candy), optional
· 6 heaped teaspoons plain yogurt

Chop the rhubarb into 1 cm/½ inch pieces and cover with sugar. Use your hands to work the sugar into the rhubarb, then leave in the refrigerator overnight to macerate. The sugar will dissolve and release the juice.

Transfer to a blender and blitz until liquidised. Tip into a tall jug and refrigerate overnight. The liquid will separate out and the vegetable matter will rise to the surface. Skim it away and pour the clear, pink juice into an ice cream machine. Churn according to the manufacturer's directions. Scoop into small serving glasses and freeze until required (up to 2 days).

To make the burnt cream, first have a large bowl set over ice in your sink. Pour the cream into a pan. Split the vanilla bean lengthwise and scrape the seeds into the cream. Heat to simmering point then remove from the heat.

Meanwhile, whisk the egg yolks with the sugar until pale and fluffy. Slowly pour the hot cream onto the egg yolk mixture, whisking slowly. Do this gradually, as if you were adding oil to a mayonnaise. Keep whisking until it begins to thicken. Pour into the bowl set over ice and stir gently while it cools. Pour into a jug and leave for 30 minutes. Pour into 6 espresso cups and tap gently to remove any air bubbles. Keep refrigerated until needed.

To make the shortbread, preheat the oven to 180°C/350°F. Combine the flours, salt and butter in a food processor and pulse to the texture of breadcrumbs. Mix in the sugar. Tip into a 28 x 19 cm/11 ¼ x 7 ½ inch non-stick baking pan. It will be rather dry and crumbly, so pack it in tightly. Bake for 20 minutes, or until the top is beginning to turn golden.

Remove from the oven and allow to cool in the pan for 30 minutes. Cut into fingers. It can be made ahead and stored in an airtight container for 2 days.

Twenty minutes before you are ready to serve, transfer the glasses of rhubarb sorbet to the refrigerator to allow it to soften a little.

Remove the burnt creams from the refrigerator. Dust the surface of each with a teaspoon of caster (superfine) sugar and use a blow torch to caramelise. Arrange the burnt creams and sorbet on attractive serving platters. Top each sorbet with a teaspoon of space dust and finish with a spoonful of yogurt. Arrange a slice of shortbread alongside and serve straight away.

The
Orchards

Tenyham Orchards
and Strawberry Fields

Teynham Orchards and Strawberry Fields

A lot of visitors to The Sportsman make the train journey from London to Faversham, and a few have commented on how the journey through the countryside resembles an advert for the food they are about to eat. As the train makes its way out of the capital from St Pancras it hurtles across the north Kent marshes in what can often appear to be quite a desolate landscape.

Then, after a while, you start to see the hop fields appear and later apple, pear and cherry orchards. As the train nears Faversham, the strawberry fields come into view, although more often than not these days they are covered in polythene during the summer to protect them from the birds and changeable weather.

The 10-minute taxi ride from Faversham station is like a short re-run of the train trip as you pass hop fields, strawberry and raspberry fields, a cherry orchard and finally appear on the Graveney Marsh that is home to The Sportsman with the sea just beyond.

Kent has been an important grower of fruit for many years. Back in 1535 Henry VIII financed large orchards to be started near the village of Teynham; I suspect it was to make up for the displaced monks who had been growing a lot of fruit before he dissolved the monasteries in that year. The reason the fruit thrives in Kent is the amount of sunlight that it is exposed to and the marginally warmer temperatures in this corner of the country.

As children and teenagers, fruit was a very important part of growing up in the area; my friends and I would earn money in the summer holidays by following the fruit-picking season. We started by picking the first crop of strawberries in June – just in time for Wimbledon – and would then pick apples from July. I still can't walk past an early Worcester or Discovery apple without the smell sending me back to hot summer days spent in the orchards. We were useless at making any money because it was piece work and you had to fill a massive wooden box for £15. The local women would fill three in a day to our one, although they did have extra help from their young children.

The end of the summer would see the hop harvest arrive, where you could earn enough to pay off your overdraft before returning to university in the autumn. Although hops paid well, you had to start at 6.30am and keep working until the light faded. The pungent smell of them got everywhere, too, and most of my friends' cars smelt of hops until Christmas.

I didn't give any of these things much thought in the years I lived in London. It wasn't until I came back to open a restaurant that I was thankful for having grown up in a place that was so connected to food and the land. Those early encounters with the agriculture of the area have been helpful in me knowing the seasons and influential in the type of food that I cook.

Smoked mackerel with cream cheese, apple jelly and soda bread with mackerel velouté

For the first six months after we opened The Sportsman I was working on my own and I often forgot to eat. (When you are surrounded by food, and tasting everything, it is easy not to get hungry.) By about midnight I would be ravenous, but couldn't ever be bothered to make anything substantial. And so I would raid the refrigerator! I lived above the restaurant, and had everything available to me, but somehow I was always drawn to soda bread and smoked eel. My favourite after-work snack was soda bread spread with cream cheese, topped with eel and horseradish sauce. One day when I was trying to dream up new starters for the menu, I remembered my midnight feasts and it didn't take long for this recipe to emerge. I replaced the eel with smoked mackerel and all that it needed then was the acidity of apple jelly to set the whole thing alight. We serve rhubarb jelly in the spring, gooseberry in the summer, crab apple in the autumn and apple for the rest of the year.

Serves 4

· 2 whole smoked mackerel fillets, skinned, filleted and flaked
· 4 slices Soda Bread [pp. 232]
· 2 tablespoons cream cheese
· Apple Jelly [pp. 242], to serve
· 4 large sorrel leaves, finely shredded, to serve
· fresh horseradish root, grated, to serve

Smoked mackerel velouté
· 1 litre (34 fl oz/4 cups) full-fat (whole) milk
· smoked mackerel bones from about 10 fish
· 2 onions, diced
· 6 celery sticks, diced
· 2 large potatoes, peeled and diced
· 2 tablespoons unsalted butter
· 1 squeeze of lemon juice
· scant 1 tablespoon sea salt
· finely chopped chives, to serve

To make the velouté, pour the milk over the bones in a saucepan and bring to a simmer. Cook for 20 minutes to extract the flavour.

Meanwhile, sweat the diced vegetables in the butter in a large saucepan for around 5 minutes.

Strain the milk over the vegetables and simmer for 5 minutes. Blitz in a blender and pass through a fine sieve, then check the seasoning and adjust with lemon and salt.

Spread each slice of soda bread generously with cream cheese. Top with a spoonful of apple jelly then cover the surface with flakes of the smoked mackerel. Finish with shredded sorrel and a little grated horseradish. Divide the smoked mackerel velouté among 4 espresso cups, top with chives and serve.

Duck with cherries

Although I usually have a rule that each taste (sweet, sour etc.) should only appear once in a dish to avoid palate confusion, this is an exception. The sweetness of both the veg and cherries allows you to ponder the difference between them. They are also in season at the same time.

Serves 4

· 2 large duck breasts, scored on the skin side to prevent shrinkage
· sea salt
· 1 teaspoon duck fat
· 1 griotte onion, thinly sliced on a mandolin
· 2 cloves
· few knobs of butter
· 450 g/ 1 lb green beans or freshly podded peas
· a few drops of lime juice
· 12 cherries, pitted and halved
· 8 tender young lemon verbena leaves, bruised

Season the duck breasts well. Heat a good non-stick frying pan on a medium heat and add the duck fat. Cook the duck breasts, skin side down, for 5–7 minutes until the skin side is mahogany brown. Be patient with this. I like to weight the breasts gently with another pan to ensure they stay in contact with the heat.

Take the pan off the heat, turn the duck breasts over and leave them to finish cooking in the warm frying pan. After 10 minutes or so, once the pan has cooled, transfer the breasts to a warm plate. Season again and leave them to rest.

Drain off as much of the fat as you can (you can use this for frying potatoes), retaining the duck juices in the pan. Return to a low heat and add the onion, cloves and a knob of butter. Warm gently, then add the green beans or peas. These will only need to be warmed up, rather than cooked.

Add a few drops of lime juice and another knob of butter. Add the cherries and give the pan a shimmy to emulsify. Remove the cloves and add the lemon verbena leaves.

Divide the beans or peas and cherries among 4 warm serving plates. Carve the duck breasts into slices, allowing half a breast per person, and serve on top of the veg and cherries.

Strawberry ice cream

Because I live so close to one of the biggest strawberry growing areas in the UK, I felt I should try and develop a spectacular recipe for strawberry ice cream. What I wanted was to get as close as possible to biting into a perfect ripe strawberry as I could. The problem for the chef is that the flavour of the fruit has to fight through other ingredients – in this case, cream. To solve this problem I began by sourcing the best, ripest strawberries I could, and then I looked to emphasise the strawberry's flavour profile by using soured cream and lime for acidity and sugar for sweetness. The other flavours I detected in the fruit were a certain nuttiness (probably from the seeds) and rose. So I added a few drops of sesame oil and rosewater until I was happy with the overall taste. Although at first glance this may seem to be a simple recipe it is important to use the sweetest, ripest strawberries, which means we only serve it at the height of summer. Make sure the fruit is at room temperature before you start. This ice cream is also made special by the use of unpasteurised crème fraîche from Ottinge Court Farm Dairy. I can't think of a better pudding on a hot summer's day.

Makes 2 litres / 70 fl oz

Strawberry ice cream
· 785 g / 28 oz (3 ¼ cups) raw crème fraîche
· 350 g / 12 oz trimolene (invert sugar)
· 750 g / 1 lb 10 oz very ripe strawberries, at room temperature
· 1 teaspoon rosewater
· 1 teaspoon sesame oil
· juice of 1 lime

· single (light) cream, to serve
· strawberries, halved, to serve

Combine all the ice cream ingredients in a blender and blitz at high speed. Transfer to the refrigerator and chill for at least 30 minutes. Pour into an ice cream machine and churn according to the manufacturer's directions. Transfer to a plastic container and freeze for at least 2 hours before serving.

Spoon into glass coupes and top with a little single (light) cream, which will set hard on the surface of the ice cream, and some strawberries.

Summer fruit salad

When I first opened The Sportsman restaurant, I knew that I wanted to find the perfect way of showing off the many different fruit varieties that are grown in Kent. Summer starts in June with the early strawberries, raspberries and then cherries. The season really kicks into gear in mid-to-late July, when redcurrants, blackberries and blackcurrants start to arrive. As well as these we have early apples, plums, gooseberries, loganberries and probably some fruits I have forgotten. There is a magical week or two at the end of July and early August when almost everything is in season at the same time.

Whenever I think of fruit salad, what always comes to mind is the Nico Ladenis version. I first saw a picture of it in a magazine called *Taste* back in the early 1990s. The photo was artfully blurred as the waiter carried the beautiful dish out into the restaurant. It looked like Carmen Miranda's hat. A biscuit tuile sat in the deepest red raspberry sauce and a large scoop of vanilla ice cream provided the structure for a cascade of fruit. When I visited his restaurant I ordered this dessert and sat silent and humbled by its perfection. Just as Michel Bras' gargouillou is the ultimate way of serving vegetables so this, I believed, could be considered a fruit equivalent.

When creating my own fruit salad for the restaurant, I used Nico's clever way of dressing the fruit with a vivid green lime syrup and then I added a dash of rose water and a few drops of sesame oil to emphasise other aspects of the various fruits' flavours. My only change was the flavour of the ice cream: I wanted the freshness of verbena rather than the richness of vanilla. Although Dan, my head chef, disagreed, I had to insist.

Summer fruit salad

Really, all you have to do for this dish is choose the fruits that are
at their seasonal best.

Serves 6

· 600–700 g/1 lb 5 oz–1 lb 9
  oz summer fruits (your choice
  of strawberries, raspberries,
  loganberries, blackberries,
  redcurrants, blackcurrants,
  cherries, plums and early apples)
· few drops of sesame oil
· few drops of rosewater
· fennel pollen, lemon verbena
  leaves, rose petals, to serve
  (optional)
· 100 ml/13 ½ fl oz (scant ½ cup)
  Lime Syrup [pp. 241], to serve
· icing (confectioners') sugar, to dust

Lemon verbena ice cream
· 600 ml/21 fl oz (2 ½ cups) double
  (heavy) cream
· 400 ml/14 fl oz (1 ⅔ cups) full-fat
  (whole) milk
· 200 ml/7 fl oz (scant 1 cup) liquid
  glucose
· small handful of lemon verbena
  leaves

Tuiles
· 210 g/7 ½ oz (1 cup) egg whites
· 200 g/7 oz (2 cups) icing
  (confectioners') sugar
· 200 g/ 7 oz (1 ⅔ cups) plain
  (all-purpose) flour
· 100 g/3 ½ oz (½ cup) melted
  butter
· 1 tablespoon honey

Raspberry sauce
· 250 g/9 oz raspberries
· 50 g/2 oz (½ cup) icing
  (confectioners') sugar

To make the ice cream, combine the cream and milk in a pan and bring to
the boil. Take off the heat and stir in the liquid glucose, then add the lemon
verbena leaves. Leave to infuse overnight.

Strain to remove the lemon verbena leaves and churn the mixture in an ice
cream machine. Transfer to a container and put in the freezer to set.

To make the tuiles, place all the ingredients in a food processor and blitz
together. Set aside and leave to rest for at least 2 hours.

Preheat the oven to 160°C/320°F and line a baking sheet with greaseproof
(wax) paper or Silpat. Spoon on several well-spaced tablespoons of the tuile
batter and use the back of the spoon to spread them out to 18 cm/7 inch
rounds. Bake for around 8 minutes, or until golden.

Remove from the oven and, while still warm, mould the tuiles around the
bottom of a glass to form baskets. Otherwise you can just serve them flat.
Leave to cool on wire racks. Like pancakes, the first few never work, but don't
give up!

To make the raspberry sauce, use a fork to crush the fruit with the sugar and
then pass through a sieve. Adjust the consistency with a little water if it is
too thick.

Cut each fruit into an attractive shape, I like try to keep the natural look of
the fruit as much as possible. For example, a raspberry should be just cut in
half from pole to pole.

Transfer all the fruit to a large bowl and gently stir in the lime syrup.
Leave to macerate for 10 minutes. At the last moment add the sesame oil and
rosewater. I also like to add some small flavour bombs, such as a pinch of
fennel pollen, a lemon verbena leaf or shreds of fresh rose petal, as these are
all in season and available in my garden.

To serve, spoon a pool of raspberry sauce onto each dessert plate. Put a
scoop of ice cream into each tuile basket then pile your fruit on top. (Think
Carmen Miranda's hat!) Dust with icing (confectioners') sugar and carefully
lift the whole thing onto the plate so it sits in the centre of the sauce.

Greengage soufflé
with greengage ripple ice cream

I didn't have a soufflé on at the pub until I came across this method. It doesn't involve creme patisserie and is more like a light cooked fruit mousse, which I personally prefer to the traditional version. I find the creme pat can mask the pure fruit flavour. We make a soufflé all year round and change the flavour with the seasons. Although the Bramley apple version is the most popular because it is served the whole winter, this one is my favourite even though it is only served in early August.

Makes 4-6 25cl soufflés

Greengage purée
· 200 g / 7 oz (1 ½ cups) greengages, stones removed

Cream cheese ice cream
· 400 ml / 14 fl oz (1 ⅔ cups) Sugar Syrup [pp. 241]
· 250 ml / 8 ½ fl oz (1 cup) double cream
· 250 ml / 8 ½ fl oz (1 cup) whole milk
· 500 g / 17 ½ oz (2 ¼ cups) cream cheese

Greengage ripple
· 500g greengage purée (see method)
· 10 g / 2 teaspoons caster (superfine) sugar
· 1 teaspoon pectin

Soufflés
· 200 g / 7 oz (1 cup) egg whites
· 90 g / 3 ¼ oz (½ cup) caster (superfine) sugar, plus extra for the moulds
· 20 g / 2 tablespoons cornflour made into a paste with a little water
· 2-4 teaspoons Spinach or Parsley Purée [see pp. 244]
· Butter, for greasing

To make the greengage purée, put the fruit in a small saucepan with a splash of water and cook until softened, around 10 minutes. Allow to cool then blitz in a food processor until smooth and pass through a sieve.

To make the ice cream, in a blender jug, blitz all the ingredients until smooth. Churn in an ice cream maker and put in a container to set in the freezer.

Follow the above method to make the greengage purée for the greengage ripple, adding the sugar when cooking. Heat again and stir in the pectin. Blitz, pass and allow to cool. When the ice cream is still soft but set, stir in the purée to get the ripple.

To make the soufflé, in a saucepan, heat the greengage purée and cornflour paste and cook until thick. Leave to cool. Whisk the egg whites until frothy and then add the sugar a bit at a time. Keep whisking until they are soft peaks.

Add the spinach or parsley purée to the greengage mix and stir to incorporate. It is to colour the mix but not enough to be able to taste.

Now whisk a third of the egg whites into the greengage mix to create a loose foam into which the rest of the egg whites can be incorporated. Fold in the rest of the egg whites, keeping as much air in the mix as possible.

Lightly butter your soufflé moulds and dust with caster sugar. Fill the moulds with the mix and tap to remove any air bubbles. Flatten the tops with a hot spatula and then run a thumb around the top edge to ensure an even rise.

Cook the soufflés in a preheated 180°C/350°F oven for about 8 minutes, then serve immediately with a scoop of ice cream.

Cream cheese ice cream with pear purée and gingerbread crumbs

This would also work well with a rhubarb purée. You can make the meringue and gingerbread crumbs ahead of time and store in airtight containers.

Serves 4

Meringue
· 100 g/3 ½ oz (½ cup) egg whites
· 175 g/6 oz (¾ cup) caster (superfine) sugar

Gingerbread crumbs
· 1 Jamaica ginger cake

Pear purée
· 4 ripe Williams pears, peeled, cored and diced
· 100 ml/3 ½ fl oz (scant ½ cup) Sugar Syrup [pp. 241]
· 1 teaspoon ascorbic acid

Cream cheese ice cream
· 400 ml/14 fl oz (1 ⅔ cups) Sugar Syrup [pp. 241]
· 250 ml/9 fl oz (1 cup) double (heavy) cream, plus extra to serve
· 250 ml /9 fl oz (1 cup) full-fat (whole) milk
· 500 g/1 llb 2 oz (2 cups) cream cheese

To make the meringue, preheat the oven to 100°C/210°F and line a baking pan with greaseproof (wax) paper. Put the egg whites into a stand mixer and whisk until frothy. Add the sugar, a bit at a time, whisking until glossy. Tip into the prepared baking pan and spread into a 2 cm/¾ inch thick layer. Leave in the oven overnight. Remove from the oven and allow to cool before crumbling into rubble.

Cut the ginger cake into slices and dry in the oven overnight, along with the meringue. Once cool, crumble into powder.

To make the pear purée, cut the pears into small chunks and put into a mini food processor or jug blender. Add the sugar syrup and ascorbic acid and blitz to make a smooth purée. Refrigerate until required.

For the ice cream, combine all the ingredients in a blender and blitz at high speed. Pour into an ice cream machine and churn according to the manufacturer's directions. Transfer to a plastic container and freeze for a few hours before serving.

To serve, spoon a little pear purée into each serving bowl and arrange a large scoop of ice cream on top. Pour a little of the extra cream over the ice cream, then top with meringue rubble and gingerbread crumbs.

Chocolate mousse cake

This has been on the menu for a long time but I still can't come up with a better chocolate and raspberry dessert for the summer.

Serves 8

· 340 g / 12 oz 70% chocolate,
  roughly chopped
· 95 g / 3 ½ oz (⅓ cup) butter,
  roughly chopped
· 1 tablespoon liquid glucose
· 8 eggs, separated into whites
  and yolks
· 40 g / 1 ½ oz (¼ cup) caster
  (superfine) sugar
· sea salt
· raw cream and fresh raspberries,
  to serve
· Raspberry Sauce [pp. 210],
  to serve

Preheat the oven to 180°C / 350°F. Remove the base from a 23 cm / 9 inch springform cake pan and wrap in greaseproof (wax) paper. Fit it back into place and butter the inside of the pan well.

Put the chocolate and butter in a large mixing bowl and set it over a pan of simmering water. Once the chocolate and butter have melted, stir gently to combine.

Warm the liquid glucose so that it is runny (a few seconds in the microwave is ideal for this). Add to the melted chocolate mixture, along with the egg yolks, and stir to thoroughly combine.

Put the egg whites into a stand mixer and whisk until frothy. Add the sugar, a bit at a time, while whisking. Whisk in a good pinch of salt and continue whisking to stiff peaks.

Gently whisk a quarter of the egg whites into the chocolate mixture to slacken. Fold in the remaining egg whites gently, as you would for a mousse, keeping as much air in the mix as possible.

Pour the mixture into the prepared cake pan and give it a little shimmy so the mixture settles. Bake for 15 minutes then take out of the oven. Don't worry if it seems quite liquid as it will set firm in the refrigerator. Leave to cool at room temperature, then refrigerate.

Remove the cake from the pan and turn it over to create a smooth, attractive top surface. Serve with raw cream, fresh raspberries and raspberry sauce.

Grilled plums with plum stone ice cream and brioche

I think plums can be a forgotten fruit but they grow very well around the pub. We use different varieties depending on the time of the year. I liked the idea of extracting the flavour of the stone into the milk sorbet as it feels like you get a bit more value out of the plums and it illustrates another dimension of taste.

Serves 4

· 4 plums, stones removed
  and halved
· sugar, for dusting
· 200 ml/ 6 ¾ fl oz (¾ cup)
  Sugar Syrup [pp. 241]
· 4 slices of Brioche [pp. 234]
· 2 tablespoons vielle prune
  eau de vie
· Milk Sorbet [pp. 160]

Follow the milk sorbet recipe, but first add the cracked plum stones to the milk and heat. Leave the stones in the milk overnight to absorb the almondy taste. The more stones you can add, the better. Finish the milk sorbet according to the recipe.

Leave the stoned plums to macerate in the sugar syrup overnight in the fridge.

To cook the dish, remove the plums from the sugar syrup and allow the plums to warm up.

Put the veille prune in a bowl – do this to taste as it depends on how boozy you want it to be – and add some of the plum flavoured sugar syrup. Soak the slices of brioche.

Dip the plums in some sugar and grill. You can do this by either grilling on a salamander or with a blowtorch. The sugar should be crisp when it cools like the top of a burnt cream.

Place a slice of brioche on each serving plate and top with a scoop of milk sorbet. Place two plum halves on each plate, drizzle with the brioche soaking liquid and serve.

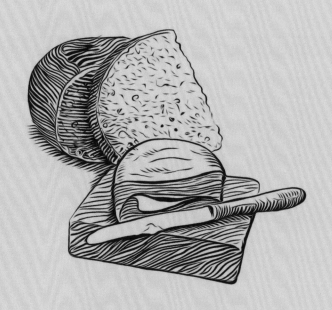

The Basics

The Sportsman Kitchen Essentials

The Sportsman Kitchen Essentials

As a self-taught chef, I am in an interesting position when writing these recipes, in that books were very important to me when I was learning how to cook. I worked my way through *Mastering the Art of French Cooking*, Nico's *My Gastronomy*, *White Heat*, *Roast Chicken and Other Stories* and many others to teach myself how to cook to a high standard.

Although I learned a huge amount, I was always aware that the books didn't follow the exact same processes that would be used to create them in a professional kitchen. As an obsessive, I wanted to go beyond adaptations suitable for domestic cooks. I wanted to know the exact way a restaurant kitchen did it and to reproduce the dish at home, and so I have tried to explain exactly how we work, but still make the recipes for the home cook.

I'll admit that another pet hate was cross-referencing in a cookbook, yet here I am, inflicting this same thing on my readers.

The only way I can explain why this is necessary is by explaining how we work. When I am developing new dishes, I tend to use whatever is around me. For example, when putting together the mussel and bacon chowder, I wanted to add some acidity and so I had the scallop roe powder to hand. The same roe powder appears in other recipes, such as the raw scallops. It is part of our kitchen's palette of tastes and it gives each chef's food a different emphasis. However, is it worth making the scallop roe powder just as a small part of the chowder recipe? If I'm honest, I would think not, but then at the same time, I remember how determined I was to exactly recreate a dish I had eaten in a restaurant – so I'll leave it up to the individual.

These basics are what will always be available in the kitchen for added seasoning, or what will appear on the table when you sit down.

Homemade butter

Double (heavy) cream will produce sweet butter and crème fraîche will produce a more lactic, acidic butter.

Makes about 600 g/ 1 lb 5 oz butter

· 1 litre/ 34 fl oz (4 cups) very good quality double (heavy) cream or 1 kg/ 2 lb 4 oz (4 cups) crème fraîche
· 6–9 g/ ⅛–¼ oz sea salt

Put the bowl of a stand mixer into the refrigerator to chill. Put the cream or crème fraîche into the cold bowl and beat at high speed with the paddle attachment. After about 5 minutes the cream will really stiffen up and you will hear a splashing sound as the butter separates out from the buttermilk.

At this stage I turn down the speed and cover the bowl loosely to prevent liquid spraying everywhere. Continue beating until the buttermilk and butterfat separate completely. Be patient as it may take another 5 minutes.

Turn off the machine and strain off the buttermilk. Rinse under cold running water and strain again. With the machine on its lowest setting, beat in the salt until fully incorporated.

Knead the butter between two pieces of wax (greaseproof) paper to squeeze out the last of the buttermilk. Finally, shape into a cylinder or a round pat, wrap in wax (greaseproof) paper and store in the refrigerator.

Seaweed butter

This is the amount of butter we make at the restaurant. It keeps well in the refrigerator for up to a week and freezes very well, but you can also scale down the recipe to your needs.

Makes about 1.5 kg/3 lb 5 oz

· 100 g/3 ½ oz fresh gutweed or sea lettuce (enough for 20 g/¾ oz dried seaweed)
· 2.5 kg/5 lb 8 oz (10 cups) crème fraiche, chilled
· 22.5 g/¾ oz (4 ½ teaspoons) sea salt

After gathering the seaweed, wash it very carefully and then dehydrate for 3 hours at 80°C/175°F. Check carefully for any shells or foreign objects, then put into a food processor and pulse to small, rough flakes. Store in an air-tight container.

Put the bowl of a stand mixer into the refrigerator to chill. Put the cream or crème fraîche into the cold bowl and beat at high speed with the paddle attachment. After about 5 minutes the cream will really stiffen up and you will hear a splashing sound as the buttermilk separates out from the buttermilk.

At this stage I turn down the speed and cover the bowl loosely to prevent liquid spraying everywhere. Continue beating until the buttermilk and butterfat separate completely. Be patient as it may take another 5 minutes or so.

Turn off the machine and strain off the buttermilk. Rinse under cold running water and strain again. With the machine on its lowest setting, mix in the salt and dried seaweed until fully incorporated.

Knead the butter between two pieces of wax (greaseproof) paper to squeeze out the last of the buttermilk. Finally, shape into a cylinder or a round pat, wrap in wax (greaseproof) paper and store in the refrigerator.

Smoked salt butter

This is also really good with grilled and pan-fried meat.

Makes about 1.5 kg/3 lb 5 oz

· 2.5 kg/5 lb 8 oz (10 cups) crème fraîche
· smoked salt
· 30 g/1 oz (2 tablespoons) Smoked Red Pepper Powder [pp. 247] or espelette pepper

Put the crème fraîche a into a smoker and leave overnight, or for a minimum of 10 hours. After smoking the crème fraîche, refrigerate until cold. At the same time, put the bowl of a stand mixer into the refrigerator to chill.

The next day, make butter from the smoked crème fraîche. Put the cold crème fraîche into the cold bowl and beat at high speed with the paddle attachment. After about 5 minutes the cream will really stiffen up and you will hear a splashing sound as the butter separates out from the buttermilk.

At this stage I turn down the speed and cover the bowl loosely to prevent liquid spraying everywhere. Continue beating until the buttermilk and butterfat separate completely. Be patient as it may take another 5 minutes or so.

Turn off the machine and strain off the buttermilk. Rinse under cold running water and strain again. With the machine on its lowest setting, beat in the smoked salt and smoked red pepper until fully incorporated.

Knead the butter between two pieces of wax (greaseproof) paper to squeeze out the last of the buttermilk. Finally, shape into a cylinder or a round pat, wrap in wax (greaseproof) paper and store in the refrigerator.

Salt

You will be left with some grey, sludgy salt in the pan – sel gris – which is great for seasoning soups and vegetable cooking water.

Makes around 300 g/ 11 oz (1 ¼ cups) salt

· 10 litres/ 2 gallons seawater (about 2 small buckets)

Collect the seawater in buckets, by skimming from the surface of the water. It helps if you have a nice calm day but it is not essential. Leave the water in the bucket for a day, so that any bits will settle at the bottom.

Carefully strain the water into large stainless steel pans using a sieve or colander lined with a J Cloth. Leave any grit at the bottom of the bucket.

Boil the water until it has almost completely evaporated and there are just a couple of inches left in the pan.

Transfer the water to a stainless-steel frying pan and put on a low heat. As the water simmers gently, white crystals will begin to form on the surface. Take the pan off the heat and skim them away. Leave the crystals to dry on a chopping board. Repeat this process three times. Once dry, transfer the white salt crystals to a sealable container to store.

Focaccia

It may seem strange that we make focaccia in a restaurant that highlights English food, but this bread is on the menu for sentimental reasons. Just before opening The Sportsman I visited The Walnut Tree restaurant in Wales. I was impressed by many things, but the bread board knocked me out: it had a cheese bread, black bread and this focaccia.

Makes 1 loaf

· 20 g/¾ oz fresh yeast
· 700 g/1 lb 9 oz (5 ½ cups) bread flour
· 20 g/¾ oz (1 tablespoon) sea salt
· 15 g/½ oz (1 tablespoon) caster (superfine) sugar
· olive oil
· 1 red onion, thinly sliced
· 2 stalks rosemary, picked into small sprigs

Crumble the fresh yeast into a bowl and pour over 500 ml/17 fl oz (generous 2 cups) warm water. Leave for 30 minutes to give the yeast time to activate.

Meanwhile, put the flour, salt and sugar into the bowl of a stand mixer fitted with a bread hook. If kneading by hand, combine in a large mixing bowl. With the mixer on a medium setting, add the yeast and water mixture to the dough and knead for around 5 minutes. The dough should be shiny and spring back when pressed with a finger; this means the glutens are in line. Leave the dough in the mixing bowl and allow to rise for an hour.

While the dough is rising, take a deep baking tin, around 30 x 24 cm/12 x 9 ½ inches and oil it very generously.

Knock the air out of the dough and turn out onto a floured work counter. Knead the dough for around 5 minutes to get it back to the shiny stage.

Swirl the oil in the pan to make sure all the inside surfaces are well-oiled. Put the dough into the pan and press into the sides and corners. Turn it over so that it is completely coated with oil. Spread the onion slices over the surface and tuck in the rosemary sprigs, distributing them evenly.

Leave for 2 hours, loosely covered with a tea towel, until the dough has risen almost to the top of the tin. Preheat the oven to 250°C/500°F.

Bake for about 45 minutes, or until the focaccia is golden brown. In the restaurant, we turn it upside down in the pan and bake for another 10 minutes to ensure it is evenly browned all over, but this is cosmetic rather than essential.

Turn out the focaccia onto a wire rack and leave for at least an hour before slicing.

Soda bread

During the 1980s my Dad lived in Dublin and when I used to visit him we always ate the local soda bread. It left a lasting impression on me and I now use it for some snacks and starters, as well as serving it on our bread board. I have seen many customers eating this bread with our butter and not wanting to move on. This version is based on Richard Corrigan's recipe but over time we have added more treacle.

Makes 1 loaf

· 125 g/4 1/2 oz (1 cup) wholemeal (whole wheat) flour
· 65 g/2 ½ oz (½ cup) self-raising flour
· 65 g/2 ½ oz (⅔ cup) pinhead oats
· 30 g/1 ¼ oz (⅓ cup) bran
· 15 g/½ oz (3 tablespoons) wheatgerm
· 1 teaspoon bicarbonate of soda (baking soda)
· 1 teaspoon sea salt
· 1 tablespoon treacle
· 300 ml/10 fl oz (1 ¼ cups) buttermilk

Preheat the oven to 220°C/425°F and generously flour a baking sheet.

Mix all the dry ingredients together in a large bowl. Add the treacle and buttermilk and mix together until fully incorporated. You can do this in a stand mixer fitted with a dough hook or paddle at low speed.

Turn the sticky dough out onto a well-floured work counter and knead lightly, just until no longer sticky. Form into a loaf shape and lift onto the prepared baking sheet.

Bake for 5 minutes, then lower the heat to 180°C/350°F and bake for 30–40 minutes. When the loaf is done it should sound hollow when you tap the underside. Or test with a skewer, which should come out clean when probed into the centre.

Leave the bread to cool on a wire rack.

Brioche

Use a 1.2 litre/40 fl oz non-stick loaf pan for one large brioche, or use
10 x 5 cm/4 x 2 inch mini bread pans to make six small brioches.
Keep the butter out of the refrigerator so it is very soft, which will make
it easier to work into the dough.

Makes 1 large brioche or 6 small
brioches

· 10 g/¼ oz fresh yeast
· 35 ml/1 fl oz (2 tablespoons)
  warm milk
· 15 g/½ oz (1 tablespoon) caster
  (superfine) sugar
· 250 g/9 oz (2 cups) bread flour
· 1 teaspoon sea salt
· 3 whole eggs, lightly beaten
· 175 g/6 oz (¾ cup) softened
  butter
· 2 egg yolks, lightly beaten, to glaze

Crumble the fresh yeast into a small bowl and pour on the warm milk.
Leave for 15 minutes to give the yeast time to activate. Stir in the sugar.

Meanwhile, put the flour and salt into the bowl of a stand mixer fitted with
a dough hook. With the mixer on a slow setting, add the yeast mixture and
knead until combined. Add the beaten eggs and mix in slowly. Still on slow
speed, add the soft butter, a teaspoon at a time, until fully incorporated. Leave
the dough in the mixing bowl until doubled in size. In a warm kitchen this
will take 1–2 hours.

Knock the air out of the dough, cover and leave in the refrigerator for
6 hours, or leave it overnight, so it is ready to finish and bake in the morning.

Butter and flour your loaf pan (or mini pans). Remove the dough from the
refrigerator and, on a well-floured work counter, roll into three even balls
(or 18 balls for small brioches). Place in the prepared pan(s) and leave to rise
for 1–2 hours, or until doubled in size.

When ready to bake, preheat the oven to 180°C/350°F. Brush the brioche
surface with beaten egg yolk and bake for 45 minutes, or until a skewer
comes out clean.

Turn out onto a wire rack and allow to cool.

Cheese biscuits

We serve these biscuits as a snack at the beginning of the tasting menu. In the summer we fill them with tomato cream and the rest of the year we fill them with onion purée. This purée can be used in all kinds of different dishes. We call it a stock ingredient, meaning it is always available in the restaurant kitchen.

Makes 20-30

· 150 g/5 ½ oz (1 ¼ cups) plain (all-purpose) flour
· 150 g/5 ½ oz (1 ¼ cups) wholemeal (whole wheat) flour
· good pinch of sea salt
· 100 g/3 ½ oz Old Winchester cheese, grated (or use Parmesan)
· 100 g/3 ½ oz Ashmore cheese, grated (any cheddar can be used instead)
· 250 g/9 oz (1 cup) softened butter

Tomato cream
· 500 g/1 lb 2 oz cherry tomatoes
· 500 ml/17 fl oz (generous 2 cups) double (heavy) cream
· 15 g/½ oz (1 tablespoon) sea salt

Onion purée
· 1 tablespoon neutral oil
· 3 large onions, finely sliced
· 1 star anise
· sea salt
· 30 g/1 ¼ oz (2 tablespoons) butter
· 1 tablespoon sherry vinegar

For the cheese biscuits, combine the flours and salt in a large mixing bowl. Rub the cheeses and butter into the flour by hand, which produces a lighter result. Knead gently into a dough then form into a long cylinder, around 2 cm/¾ inch in diameter. Wrap in clingfilm (plastic wrap) and chill in the refrigerator for at least an hour.

Preheat heat the oven to 180°C/350°F and lightly flour a non-stick baking sheet.

Cut the chilled dough into 5 mm/¼ inch slices and arrange on the baking sheet. Bake for 12 minutes, or until light golden brown. Transfer to a wire rack and leave to cool.

To make the tomato cream, put the cherry tomatoes into a blender and blitz until smooth. Pour into a pan, bring to a boil, then simmer until reduced by half. Stir in the cream and bring back to a boil.

Remove from the heat and carefully pour the tomato cream through a sieve lined with a J Cloth. Return to the cleaned pan and simmer until it has reduced by two thirds and has a nice glossy shine. Add the salt and leave to cool slightly. Transfer the tomato cream to a piping bag and refrigerate until it has thickened up enough to pipe.

For the onion purée, heat the oil in a heavy pan. Add the onions and star anise and cook very gently for around 20 minutes, then remove the star anise. Add a pinch of salt and continue cooking slowly, stirring every now and then, for a further 30 minutes or so. The onions should gradually turn golden brown and become meltingly tender and sweet. At this point, stir in the butter and vinegar and cook for a further 10 minutes. Taste and adjust the seasoning.

Put the onions into a blender and blitz to a smooth purée. Leave to cool, then transfer to a piping bag and refrigerate until it has thickened up enough to pipe.

To serve, pipe your choice of filling onto one biscuit and sandwich with another. Serve within 15 minutes, to avoid them getting soggy.

Mashed potatoes

Serves 6

· 5 medium potatoes
· 300 ml/10 ½ fl oz (1 ¼ cups)
  double (heavy) cream
· 50 g/2 oz (¼ cup) butter
· 1 teaspoon salt

Preheat the oven to 180°C/350°F.

Roast the potatoes in their skins for 2 hours, then remove from the oven and allow to cool slightly.

Cut the potatoes in half and scoop out the flesh (use rubber gloves if they are too hot). Press the potato flesh through a ricer into a mixing bowl.

Heat the cream in a small pan and simmer for 5 minutes, taking care it doesn't catch on the bottom of the pan.

Mix the hot cream into the potato then press it through a fine sieve. Mix in the butter then season with salt and serve.

Potato gratin

Serves 6–8

· 750 ml/25 fl oz (3 cups) double
  (heavy) cream
· 1 tablespoon salt
· 2 sprigs rosemary
· 2 sprigs thyme
· 2 garlic cloves, bruised
· 5–6 medium floury potatoes,
  peeled and thinly sliced on
  a mandolin

Preheat the oven to 180°C/350°F.

In a large pan, bring the cream to a boil. Remove the pan from the heat, add the salt, rosemary, thyme and garlic and leave to infuse while you prepare the potatoes.

Layer the potatoes in a 25 x 15 x 5 cm/10 x 6 x 2 inch baking pan until half full. Pour on half the infused cream, then layer on the remaining potato slices. Pour on the remaining cream, then cover loosely with aluminium foil, to allow for any expansion by steam.

Sit the pan on a baking sheet (in case the cream bubbles over) and bake for 1 hour. Remove the foil and test with a small knife – it should meet no resistance – then return to the oven, uncovered, for a further 15 minutes, until the top is golden brown.

Fish velouté

Makes 500 ml/17 fl oz
(generous 2 cups)

· 20 g/3/4 oz butter
· 1 shallot, thinly sliced
· 250 ml/9 fl oz (1 cup) white wine
· 250 ml/9 fl oz (1 cup) vermouth
· 500 ml/17 fl oz (generous 2 cups)
  fish stock
· 500 ml/17 fl oz (generous 2 cups)
  double (heavy) cream
· lemon juice, to taste
· sea salt

Melt the butter in a pan and sauté the shallot until it is soft but not coloured.

Add the white wine and vermouth and bring to a boil. Boil until reduced to about 1 tablespoon of liquid. Add the fish stock and boil until reduced to about 2 tablespoons of liquid.

Add the cream, bring to a simmer and cook for 8 minutes.

Strain through a sieve then add lemon juice and salt to taste.

Chicken stock

Makes 2 litres/67 fl oz

· 2 kg/4lb 4 oz raw chicken
  trimmings and bones
· 2 celery sticks, roughly chopped
· 1 leek, roughly chopped
· 1 large onion, roughly chopped
· 2 carrots, roughly chopped
· 2 cloves garlic, bruised
· 1 star anise

Put the chicken trimmings and bones in large saucepan and cover with 3 litres/101 fl oz cold water. Bring to the boil and skim the scum from the surface.

Simmer for 2 hours, adding more water to keep it topped up, if needed.

Add the rough chopped veg and simmer for another hour, then strain.

Green beans

Serves 2-4

· 8 medium-size runner beans
· 1 tablespoon Lime Syrup
 [pp. 241]
· sea salt
· good squeeze of lime juice

Use a vegetable peeler to slice the runner beans lengthwise into thin strips. Place in a bowl and toss with the lime syrup and salt. Leave for at least 30 minutes, tossing occasionally. Add a good squeeze of lime juice then taste and adjust the seasoning if need be. Reserve until ready to serve.

Sautéed cabbage

Serves 4

· 1 Savoy cabbage (or another green cabbage), outer leaves discarded
· 50 g/2 oz (¼ cup) butter
· lemon juice
· sea salt and pepper

Cut the cabbage into quarters and discard the hard core sections. Cut into thin slices and wash.

Melt 20 g/¾ oz of the butter in a lidded frying pan. Add the wet cabbage, cover the pan, and cook for 2 minutes over medium heat. Remove the lid and cook for around 2 minutes, or until the water has evaporated and the cabbage is soft, but still green.

Add the remaining butter, then add lemon juice and seasoning to taste. Stir briskly to amalgamate, check the seasoning again, then serve.

Sugar syrup

Makes 350 ml/ 12 fl oz (1½ cups)

· 200 ml/ 7 fl oz (scant 1 cup) water
· 200 g/ 7 oz (1 cup) caster
  (superfine) sugar

Combine the water and sugar in a pan and boil for 10 minutes. Remove from the heat and leave to cool completely.

Lime syrup

Makes 350 ml/ 12 fl oz (1½ cups)

· 200 ml/ 7 fl oz (scant 1 cup) water
· 200 g/ 7 oz (1 cup) caster
  (superfine) sugar
· zest of 2 limes

Combine the water and sugar in a pan and boil for 10 minutes. Remove from the heat and leave to cool completely.

Once cold, add the grated lime zest to the syrup and infuse for 30 minutes, stirring occasionally. Strain through a J Cloth and store until you want to use it. It keeps well for up to a week and makes a great cordial, sauce for ice cream or cocktail mixer.

Apple sauce

Makes 600 ml/ 20 fl oz (2 ½ cups)

· 2 large Bramley apples, unpeeled, quartered and cored
· 350 ml/ 12 fl oz (1 ½ cups) Sugar Syrup [pp. 241]

To make the apple sauce, cut the apples into small chunks and put into a small food processor or jug blender. Pour in enough sugar syrup to almost cover the apples. Blitz on high until you have a smooth, bright green sauce.

Apple jelly

Makes 450 ml/ 15 fl oz (2 cups)

· 450 ml/ 15 fl oz (scant 2 cups) good quality apple juice
· 3 bronze gelatine sheets

To make the apple jelly, measure 100 ml/3 ½ fl oz (scant ½ cup) of the juice and heat in a small pan to just below boiling. Soak the gelatine sheets briefly in warm water, just until softened. Squeeze to remove excess water then add to the hot juice and allow to dissolve. Stir back into the remaining juice, then pour into a shallow container and refrigerate for at least 8 hours, until set.

Apple balsamic vinegar

Makes 100 ml/ 3 fl oz (¼ cup)

· 500 ml/ 17 fl oz (generous 2 cups) Bramley apple juice
· 2 tablespoons cider vinegar

Combine the apple juice and cider vinegar in a small pan and simmer until reduced to around 100 ml/3 ½ fl oz (scant ½ cup) of liquid. Set aside and leave to cool.

Spinach purée

Makes 500 ml/17 fl oz
(scant 2 cups)

· 1 large bunch spinach leaves,
  washed
· sea salt

Bring a large pan of water to a boil. Add the spinach and boil for around 3-5 minutes, until wilted. Drain and reserve the cooking liquid.

Transfer to a blender. Blend on low speed, adding the cooking water a tablespoon at a time, until you achieve a smooth, loose purée. (Don't add it too quickly as you don't want the purée to be too liquid.)

Push through a sieve then season with sea salt to taste. Transfer to an airtight container and refrigerate for up to 2–3 days. Cool very quickly to keep the green colour in a bowl of ice.

Parsley purée

Makes 300 ml/10 fl oz (1 ¼ cups)

· 1 large bunch parsley leaves
· sea salt

Bring a large pan of water to a boil. Snap the bottom stalks off the bunch of parsley and discard. Boil the rest of the parsley for 1 minute.

Transfer to a blender. Blend on low speed, adding the cooking water a tablespoon at a time, until you achieve a smooth, loose purée. (Don't add it too quickly as you don't want the purée to be too liquid.)

Push through a sieve then season with sea salt to taste. Transfer to an airtight container and refrigerate for up to 2–3 days. Cool very quickly to keep the green colour in a bowl of ice.

Crystallised seaweed powder

Follow the method on pp. 246 for collecting and drying seaweed but
leave in large pieces, rather than crumbling.

· dried seaweed
· egg whites, whisked until frothy
· icing (confectioners') sugar

Brush the seaweed with egg white and dust lightly with icing (confectioners') sugar. Place in a dehydrator and dry overnight at 70°C/150°F, by which time it should be crisp enough to crumble with your fingers into a sweet-umami powder. Alternatively, blitz to a powder in a coffee grinder. Store in an airtight jar until required.

Cooked crab

At The Sportsman, we cook crabs to order for our tasting menu. If you are
confident enough to do this at home, then a 2 kg/4 lb 8 oz crab should provide
sufficient white meat for 4 people (reserve the brown meat for another dish).

Serves 4

· 2 kg/4 lb 8 oz crab

Put the crab in the freezer for 20 minutes. After this time, place it on a chopping board, turn it on its back with its legs facing upward. Raise the tail flap and push a small screwdriver or skewer through the hole underneath. Press firmly down on the screwdriver handle until it hits the other side of the shell, then remove the screwdriver. Remove the crab carapace and rinse clean.

Fill a large pan with salted water (3% by weight – the same as seawater) and bring to a boil. Plunge the crab into the boiling water and cook for 20 minutes.

Once cooked, remove from the water and leave at room temperature for at least 2 hours, to cool, before picking the meat from the shell.

Seaweed powder

This is more of a guide than a definitive recipe. Making the powder will depend on the time of year, the type of seaweed and the amount you collect.

· seaweed

Go to the beach and gather gutweed and sea lettuce. Wash in many changes of fresh water until all the sand and grit is removed. Shake dry.

Arrange the seaweed in a thin layer on a baking sheet (if oven-drying) or on the shelves of a dehydrator. Dry at 70°C/150°F for around 12 hours, or until the moisture has almost entirely gone and the seaweed is crisp.

Use your fingers to crumble into a rough powder. Alternatively, blitz to a powder in a coffee grinder. Store in an airtight jar until required.

Scallop roe powder

Makes 3 tablespoons

· 12 scallop roes
· Smoked Red Pepper Powder
 [pp. 247] or Espelette pepper,
 to taste
· salt, to taste
· ascorbic acid, to taste

To make the scallop roe powder, put the roes into a dehydrator and dry overnight at 75°C/165°F. It may take longer to achieve the required crisp texture. Transfer to a coffee grinder and blitz to a powder. Sieve to remove any resistant larger bits.

The next stage requires a bit of tasting and judgement on your part. Add some chilli powder – start with around 20% of the volume of scallop roe powder. You want to be able to tell that it is there, but without overpowering the flavour of the roe. Now season with salt to taste and add enough ascorbic acid to give a bit of tanginess.

Smoked red pepper powder

Makes 100 g/ 3 ½ oz

· 30 mild red chilli peppers

Slice the chillies lengthwise and remove the seeds and white membranes. Put into a cold smoker and smoke overnight.

Transfer the smoked chillies to a dehydrator and dry for 2 days at 75°F/165°F.

When the chillies are dry enough, transfer to a coffee grinder and blitz to a powder. Sieve to remove any resistant larger bits, then return these bits to the grinder and blitz again. Store in an airtight jar until required.

Cep powder

Makes 10 g/ ¼ oz

· 10 g/ ¼ oz dried ceps

Arrange the ceps on a baking sheet and warm in a 150°C/300°F oven for 5 minutes. Transfer to a coffee grinder and blitz to a powder. Store in an airtight container until ready to serve.

My Previous with The Sportsman

1966   My first encounter with The Sportsman was when we went on a bus trip orga-nised by the local church in Sidcup, south London, to the seaside. I have very vague memories of the day as I was only five years old, but I remember my mum singing the song 'Yesterday' by The Beatles. I thought that she must be upset for some reason if she was singing such a sad song.

1968   Partly as a result of that trip in 1966, we ended up moving to Whitstable when my Dad got a job in Canterbury in 1968. A few years later Philip was cycling back from Faversham when he stopped at the pub. He asked for a drink and the barman offered lager or bitter clearly unaware that Phil was fourteen. Phil still remembers that the beer was badly kept.

1973   Our school, Queen Elizabeth's Faversham, has a sponsored walk that runs from the school to The Sportsman. This began in 1973, and Phil and I went on the first one. This walk still happens today, and it gives us great pleasure to be able to help the school with its fundraising, despite being invaded by several hundred schoolchildren. The Sportsman was always that strange place on the edge of town and we would go up onto the beach near the pub and have barbecues with a big group of friends. In those days, someone would drive his land rover on to the beach – which was possible back then – and we would cook, listen to music and drink beer all afternoon.

1978   Back in 1978, our punk band, The Ignerents, were due to make an album with Step Forward records and we were booked in to rehearse at Graveney village hall, a mile down the road from The Sportsman. The hall was legendary in local music folk-lore as the place where pioneers of the Canterbury sound, Caravan, had rehearsed and lived in tents during the hippie years. The label had been developing us for a couple of years (you can see my diary entry about band practice on pp.62) and had sent down Glenn Tilbrook of Squeeze to produce a single. They felt that we needed more help, especially with the drums, and so the label owner Miles Copeland sent his brother Stuart, drummer with an unknown band called The Police, to help develop the music for an album. He would drive down in his purple Beetle several times a week and knock the songs into shape ready for recording. We used the pub as somewhere to get a drink and discuss plans for the next day. The album project was shelved when The Police released 'Roxanne' and that was the last we saw of Stuart – at least, it was in person.

Recipe Notes

Some of the recipes require advanced techniques, specialist equipment and professional experience to achieve good results.

Exercise a high level of caution when following recipes involving any potential hazardous activity, including the use of high temperatures, open flames and when deep-frying. In particular, when deep-frying, add food carefully to avoid splashing, wear long sleeves and never leave the pan unattended.

Cooking times are for guidance only, as individual ovens vary. If using a fan (convection) oven, follow the manufacturer's instructions concerning oven temperatures.

Some recipes include raw or very lightly cooked eggs, meat, or fish and fermented products. These should be avoided by the elderly, infants, pregnant women, convalescents and anyone with an impaired immune system.

Exercise caution when making fermented products, ensuring all equipment is spotlessly clean, and seek expert advice if in any doubt.

When no quantity is specified, for example of oils, salts, and herbs used for finishing dishes or for deep-frying, quantities are discretionary and flexible.

All herbs, shoots, flowers and leaves should be picked fresh from a clean source. Exercise caution when foraging for ingredients; any foraged ingredients should only be eaten if an expert has deemed them safe to eat.

We would like to thank Hattie Ellis,
Jay Rayner, Diana Henry and Marina
O'Loughlin for their support from the
very early days.

Thanks also to Moby Pomerance,
Damian Harris, Gabrielle Harris,
Jonathan, Yvonne and Bobby Neame,
Greg Wallis and all at Shepherd Neame,
and Björn Frantzen, Bonjwing,
Ali, Tom and Beth Kerridge, Mikael
Jonsson, Andy Hayler, Emilia Terragni,
Ellie Smith, Eve O'Sullivan, Marco
Velardi and Toby Glanville.

Finally, thanks to Russel, Sean, Nick,
Trev, Lauren, Grace, Hannah, Phoebe,
Sophie, John the wash-up and everyone
at The Sportsman past and present.

The publishers would like to thank
Hilary Bird, Alison Cowan, Lucy Malouf,
João Mota, Leonardo Pertile and Ivo
Rubboli for their contributions to
the book.

Phaidon Press Limited
Regent's Wharf
All Saints Street
London N1 9PA

Phaidon Press Inc.
65 Bleecker Street
New York, NY 10012

phaidon.com

First published 2017
© 2017 Phaidon Press Limited

ISBN 978 0 7148 7495 1

A CIP catalogue record for this book is
available from the British Library and
the Library of Congress.

Publisher: Emilia Terragni
Commissioning Editor: Ellie Smith
Senior Editor: Eve O'Sullivan
Production Controller: Joe Kaler

Designed by Apartamento Studios

Illustrations by Jaume Vilardell

Photographs by Toby Glanville

Printed in China